"Simple and straightforward, Meet Me in the Bible is a wonderful resource to gain foundational skills in studying the Bible. If you want to feel confident in mining Scripture for God's truths and applying it to your life, this is an incredible guide."

Laura Wifler, Cofounder, Risen Motherhood; coauthor, *Risen Motherhood: Gospel Hope for Everyday Moments*

"I was greeted by the bright smile of Colleen Searcy over thirty years ago when I walked into a youth group in West Texas as a freckle-faced, curly headed, unbelieving teenager. Over the last three decades, I have watched Colleen cling to God's word, teach God's word, sing God's word, and live God's word. If you are looking to *meet* God in the Scriptures, I can think of no better guide than my friend Colleen. She will help you taste and see that the Lord is good!"

Shane Barnard, singer-songwriter, Shane and Shane

"Colleen Searcy is one of my favorite Bible teachers. You will sense her open-armed ministry within the framework of her Meet Me in the Bible series, in which she's thoughtfully prepared a table for women to feast on God's word. Whether you are an individual hungry to know God more, a small group desiring an accessible way to study together, or a women's ministry leader looking for a foundational resource for your teaching team, the Meet Me in the Bible series is a trustworthy guide."

Caroline Saunders, author, *Come Home: Tracing God's Promise of Home through Scripture*

"I've benefited from Colleen's wisdom, teaching, and partnership in ministry for a number of years. She is a gifted Bible teacher who uses her skills to invite others into biblical literacy. In the Meet Me in the Bible series, she provides what few studies do—an opportunity for women to gather for both in-person teaching and discussion. You will be equipped to not only study for yourself but also cultivate teaching gifts in the lives of the women in your church. I can't wait to recommend this to my ministry friends."

Courtney Reissig, author, *Teach Me to Feel: Worshiping through the Psalms in Every Season of Life*

"As the CEO of a worldwide mission agency, I highly recommend Colleen Searcy's Meet Me in the Bible series for anyone interested in going deeper in their study of the Bible. Colleen uses a structured approach with guiding prompts that are fully interactive and enhance your reflection on Scripture. These books are helpful resources for pursuing individual study or leading a Bible study group, and these studies are culturally relevant for all groups of people. Meet Me in the Bible is an excellent and well-rounded framework that can make studying the Bible a more engaging and enriching experience for anyone."

Kurt Nelson, CEO, East-West Ministries

"I have seen firsthand the fruit of Meet Me in the Bible. Colleen's accessible framework for studying the Scripture has had a large and lasting impact on our church. Many in our congregation are still reaping the benefits of her investment in our women's ministry. If you are a seasoned student of the Scripture or are just getting started, Meet Me in the Bible will launch you into a greater exploration of the Bible and a deeper enjoyment of the God it reveals."

JR Vassar, Lead Pastor, Church at the Cross, Grapevine, Texas; author, *Glory Hunger*

THE STORY OF JACOB

Meet Me in the Bible Studies

Colossians and Philemon

The Stories of Women

The Story of Abraham

The Story of Jacob

MEET ME IN THE BIBLE

THE STORY OF JACOB

AN 8-WEEK BIBLE STUDY

COLLEEN D. SEARCY

Foreword by Jen Wilkin

WHEATON, ILLINOIS

The Story of Jacob: An 8-Week Bible Study

Published by Crossway
1300 Crescent Street
Wheaton, Illinois 60187

Tool 1, "Bible Timeline," designed by Brooke Hawkins.

Definitions in Tool 4, "The Attributes of God," are taken from or informed by *The ABCs of God* by Jill Nelson. © 1998, 2016 Jill Nelson. Illustrations Truth78.org. All rights reserved. Used by permission.

Cover illustration and design by Brooke Hawkins

First printing 2025

Printed in China

Trade paperback ISBN: 978-1-4335-9690-2
ePub ISBN: 978-1-4335-9692-6
PDF ISBN: 978-1-4335-9691-9

Crossway is a publishing ministry of Good News Publishers.

RRD 34 33 32 31 30 29 28 27 26 25
15 14 13 12 11 10 9 8 7 6 5 4 3 2 1

CONTENTS

FOREWORD

For the past twenty-five years, my primary place of ministry has been the local church, and my primary aim has been to build Bible literacy among women. So, naturally, any time I'm asked to endorse a resource, I ask myself how it will serve that context. That's why I'm particularly excited to bring to your attention the Meet Me in the Bible series.

When evaluating a resource, I hold two important questions in view: (1) Is this from a trustworthy voice? and (2) Does this challenge those who use it to grow in their ability to read and understand the Scriptures? I want to help answer both of those questions for you as you consider how the Meet Me in the Bible series might help you personally, or those you serve in your church.

In terms of the trustworthiness of the author, I can speak with confidence that Colleen Searcy is an excellent guide. I first met Colleen in 2008, about a year after moving to Dallas and joining a new church. I was looking for other women in the church who shared my desire to see women equipped with solid discipleship opportunities. Colleen and I went to coffee, and I knew I had found a like-minded partner. Since that time, we have together taught, written curriculum, led teams, and prayed—all from that desire to see God's daughters grounded in the Scriptures. Colleen is not only theologically and biblically solid; she is a gifted teacher, humble and kind, and a faithful friend.

In terms of the usefulness of the resource, Meet Me in the Bible so closely aligns with my own philosophy of teaching that I can recommend it eagerly. It's a brilliant combination of a Scripture journal and a guide for growing in Bible literacy. It encourages the user to practice the time-tested method of "observe, interpret, apply" in a way that allows understanding to grow gradually. It presses us to be active learners rather than passive consumers, not rushing to commentaries, but sitting with the text, patiently waiting for our own understanding to begin to emerge. For those who know my method and Bible studies, Meet Me in the Bible will feel familiar in the best ways.

It is a streamlined approach suitable for personal study as well as an excellent foundation for group discussion and teaching environments.

The skills taught in each Meet Me in the Bible study will help you understand a particular book of the Bible better. But they will also help you understand *any* book of the Bible better as you grow in your ability to use those skills. And because application focuses on relationship—with God, self, and others—these skills will help you to live and love like a Christ follower.

So it is my pleasure to commend to you both a trusted guide and a trustworthy resource. My guess is that if you had come to coffee with Colleen and me on that day some years ago, you would have shared our excitement to see women growing in their love of the Scriptures and of the God they proclaim. What we want for you is to be able to serve your local church, whether in a classroom or a living room, with good tools and the confidence to use them. My prayer is that you would take what Colleen has created and combine it with an invitation to the women God has placed in your sphere of influence—a simple invitation: Meet me in the Bible! No sweeter fellowship is found than in that meeting place. May your time spent there yield the richest of treasures.

JEN WILKIN
Bible teacher; author, *Women of the Word*;
None Like Him; and *In His Image*

MEET ME IN THE BIBLE

A Simple Framework for Reading the Bible and Enjoying God

God delights in revealing himself, and one of the primary ways he reveals himself is through the Bible. My deep desire is for people to know and enjoy God through the study of his word. I want people with all kinds of personalities and learning styles to grow in confidence that they can read and study their Bibles. This framework of Bible study was designed to provide helpful structure and a lot of freedom for the studier.

The *Why* behind Meet Me in the Bible

Meet Me in the Bible is a simple, five-step framework designed to help you read your Bible. It is not a fill-in-the-blank study. After numerous conversations with women over many years of ministry, I've found that countless women do Bible studies, yet few feel confident opening the Bible and reading it on their own. And although many women desire to lead a Bible study, few feel equipped to do so. Meet Me in the Bible offers a method to help you do both.

How to Use Meet Me in the Bible

This framework was designed for either individual or group Bible study, and it incorporates the time-tested stages of Bible reading: observation, interpretation, and application. Prompts are provided on your bookmark to help you observe, interpret, and apply the Scriptures. You will also be prompted to use simple and accessible tools as you study. You will grow in confidence and find your pace as you practice observing, interpreting, and applying the Scriptures again and again. You can use this framework to study any book of the Bible.

For Group Study

If you are doing this study as part of a group, you will want to complete each lesson before you meet. Each lesson is divided into five doable steps rather than five assigned days, to allow flexibility. You can work through one step each day or the whole lesson in one sitting. Find the pace that works best for you. No matter how much of the lesson you are able to complete, please don't skip gathering with your Bible study group. You will benefit from your group, and your group will be encouraged by your presence.

Meet Me in the Bible studies are meant to be flexible. Group studies can opt to meet in small groups for discussion and a time of teaching or simply meet for discussion only.

TIPS FOR GROUPS THAT OPT TO MEET FOR BOTH A TIME OF DISCUSSION AND A TIME OF TEACHING

- If this is your group's first Meet Me in the Bible study, be sure each participant is familiar with how to use the Meet Me in the Bible framework before you meet. You can find my videos on how to use the Meet Me in the Bible framework at colleensearcy.com/mmibteaching. In these videos, I demonstrate how to cross-reference, quickly check other translations, and more, using simple and free digital tools.

- For the first meeting, teachers will want to cover the Getting Started section before discussion. One of the greatest Bible study tools available is the historical context of the Bible book you are studying. To have the best chance of interpreting the Scriptures correctly, you need to know who the author was, whom he was writing to, the literary style he used, and what was happening in the world when he wrote it. I cover the answers to these questions in my "Getting Started" video, which you will find at colleensearcy.com/mmibteaching.

- After answering those preliminary questions, move to small-group discussion. Spend time getting to know one another. You can use the Getting Started questions in Tool 7 of the Tool Kit.

- For all future meetings, you can gather for discussion before or after the teaching. I suggest that you gather *before* the teaching. You will be amazed at the insights gained as each participant shares what was discovered during personal study. Confidence will grow as you learn from one another's discoveries. Tips for discussion:

  - The prompts on your bookmark make good points of discussion. (What did you learn from the repeated words? What was hard to understand? What did you learn about people?)
  - Content-specific discussion questions for each lesson can be found in Tool 7 of the Tool Kit.
  - Additional historical context is given in the questions in Tool 7 of the Tool Kit.
  - The bounce questions in Tool 7 of the Tool Kit are intended to jumpstart discussion and provide an easy transition to the content.
  - Discussion leaders may use as many or as few discussion questions from Tool 7 as they'd like. These questions were written to help you think deeply about the text. Many of the questions do not have one right answer and are meant to encourage further thought and robust discussion. Questions with one correct answer (e.g., What did Paul say about sin in verse 12?) can feel like a quiz rather than an invitation into conversation.

- Discussion leaders *do* want to plan which questions they will cover and think through their own answers before the group meets. They *do not* need to feel pressure to answer every question that surfaces during Bible study. The purpose of Bible study is not to impress with our knowledge; it is to grow in our knowledge of and love for God as we get to know him better through the study of his word. Enjoy being a colearner with those you are studying alongside. If the questions that surface are not answered in the teaching time, you can circle back with your group after you've had time to think further about them.

- Use the prayer pages in Tool 6 of the Tool Kit to record personal prayer requests and the prayers of those you are studying alongside.

TIPS FOR GROUPS THAT OPT TO MEET FOR DISCUSSION ONLY

- If this is your group's first Meet Me in the Bible study, be sure each participant watches my videos on how to use the Meet Me in the Bible framework before you meet. You can find them at colleensearcy.com/mmibteaching. In these videos, I demonstrate how to cross-reference, quickly check other translations, and more, using simple and free digital tools.
- For the first meeting, be prepared to discuss the Getting Started section. One of the greatest Bible study tools available is the historical context of the Bible book you are studying. To have the best chance of interpreting the Scriptures correctly, you need to know who the author was, whom he was writing to, the literary style he used, and what was happening in the world when he wrote it. I answer these questions in my "Getting Started" video at colleensearcy.com/mmibteaching.
- Spend time getting to know one another. You can use the Getting Started questions in Tool 7 of the Tool Kit.
- For all future meetings:
    - The prompts on your bookmark make good points of discussion: What did you learn from the repeated words? What was hard to understand? What did you learn about people?
    - Content-specific discussion questions for each lesson can be found in Tool 7 of the Tool Kit.
    - The bounce questions in Tool 7 of the Tool Kit are intended to jumpstart discussion and provide an easy transition to the content.

- Additional historical context is given in the questions found in Tool 7 of the Tool Kit.
- Discussion leaders may use as many or as few discussion questions from Tool 7 as they'd like. These questions were written to help you think deeply about the text. Many of the questions do not have one right answer and are meant to encourage further thought and robust discussion. Questions with one correct answer (e.g., What did Paul say about sin in verse 12?) can feel like a quiz rather than an invitation into conversation.

- Discussion leaders *do* want to plan on which questions they will cover and think through their own answers before the group meets. They *do not* need to feel pressure to answer every question that surfaces during Bible study. The purpose of Bible study is not to impress with our knowledge; it is to grow in our knowledge of and love for God as we get to know him better through the study of his word. When stumped by a question, you can say something like, "That is a great question! I'd like to give that more thought and circle back next time we meet." Then have fun studying! Enjoy being a colearner with those you are studying alongside. Ask God to help you with the questions that surface. He is delighted to meet you in the Bible. What a great discussion you will have the next time you meet!
- Use the prayer pages in Tool 6 of the Tool Kit to record personal prayer requests and the prayers of those you are studying alongside.

For Individual Study

- If you are doing this study on your own, you will want to begin by watching my videos on how to use the Meet Me in the Bible framework. You can find them at colleensearcy.com/mmibteaching. In these videos, I demonstrate how to cross-reference, quickly check other translations, and more, using simple and free digital tools.

- Be sure to complete the Getting Started section before diving in to study the passages of Scripture. One of the greatest Bible study tools available is the historical context of the Bible book you are studying. When you study a passage that is hard to understand, overlay the passage with the context. To have the best chance of interpreting the Scriptures correctly, we need to know who the author was, whom he was writing to, the literary style he used, and what was happening in the world when he wrote it. I answer these questions in my "Getting Started" video at colleensearcy.com/mmibteaching.
- After completing the Getting Started section, each lesson is divided into five doable steps rather than five assigned days, to allow flexibility. You can work through one step each day or work through the whole lesson in one sitting. Find the pace that works best for you.
- For a deeper dive, use the questions in Tool 7 of the Tool Kit. Additional historical context is also given within the questions. These questions were written to help you think deeply about the text.
- Use the prayer pages in Tool 6 of the Tool Kit to record your prayers while you study.

What's Included in This Study

Bible Study Bookmark

All Meet Me in the Bible studies include a bookmark with the time-tested stages of Bible reading (Observe, Interpret, and Apply) on the front. You will see the five-step framework for reading the Bible on the back of the bookmark, including prompts to help you observe, interpret, and apply the Scriptures. You will also be prompted to pause in your study to listen to and enjoy God. He wants to meet you in your study of the Bible! Although the Bible study bookmark and the Bible study book were designed to work together, your bookmark can also be used alone. It was designed to help you study any book of the Bible, and my hope is that you will use your bookmark again and again.

Bible Study Book

The book includes word-for-word Bible text. Mark it up! If you love highlighters, highlight away! If you prefer to draw symbols, grab colored pencils and go for it. Or simply underline with your favorite pen. Your Bible study book also includes titles and designated spaces that correspond with the titles and prompts on your bookmark. Additionally, you will find blank note pages throughout your book to use as you wish. Draw a chart, sketch an image, or write the lyrics to a song. Each lesson concludes with an important wrap-up question to prompt you to consider what you discovered in the Scriptures.

Meet Me in the Bible Tool Kit

Tool 1: *Bible Timeline*. Understanding historical context is key to reading and interpreting the Scriptures. Place an *X* on the simple timeline of the Bible to indicate where the scriptures you are studying land in the whole story of the Bible.

Tool 2: *Map*. Referencing a map while studying is a helpful reminder that these are stories of real people in real places.

Tool 3: *Bible Genres*. Knowing the literary style of the book of the Bible you are studying is key to correct interpretation. Just as you would approach the poems of Wordsworth differently than you would approach a history book about World War II, there are nuances to different literary styles in the Bible that must be kept in mind while interpreting and applying the Scriptures. Use this resource to identify the literary style of the book you are studying.

Tool 4: *Attributes of God*. You will be prompted to use this tool each week. You may want to mark it with a paper clip so you can turn there easily. The ultimate goal of Bible study is to know and love God, and my prayer is that your hope will be further anchored in him as you are reminded of his attributes.

Tool 5: *Bookmark Content*. All the information on your bookmark is included here for your convenience.

Tool 6: *Prayer Pages*. Use these pages to record personal prayers and prayer requests of those studying alongside you.

Tool 7: *Questions for Further Thought and Discussion.* Use as many or as few of these questions as you'd like in your individual or group study. Additional historical context is included in the questions. The bounce questions are intended to jumpstart discussion and provide an easy transition to the content. The remaining questions were written to help you think deeply about the text.

Additional Tools for Your Study

1. *Different Bible translations.* Reading Scripture verses in different Bible translations can give helpful insight as you study. This book includes the ESV translation. Other translations I recommend are the New International Version (NIV), the New Living Translation (NLT), the Christian Standard Bible (CSB), and the New American Standard Bible (NASB). I use The Message as a commentary when I study.

2. *Dictionary and thesaurus.* Look up unfamiliar words as well as "church" words such as *atonement*, *propitiation*, and *covenant*. You will be surprised how much clarity can be gained by reading simple definitions and synonyms in a dictionary or thesaurus.[1]

3. *Cross-references.* Cross-references are included in study Bibles, usually in the middle or at the bottom of a page. A cross-reference is a marker in the Bible pointing to other passages of Scripture with related words and themes. It is usually designated with a superscript (tiny, raised) letter. Cross-referencing is a way to use Scripture to rightly interpret Scripture. You can also use digital tools to cross-reference.[2]

4. *Study Bible footnotes.* If you have a study Bible, the provided footnotes give helpful insights.[3] Wait to check footnotes until after you've observed the text and attempted interpretation using other translations, a dictionary, and cross-references, and overlaying the passage with the context. Resist the temptation to jump to someone else's thoughts before observing and interpreting on your own. Enjoy being curious and see what you discover!

5. *Commentaries.* Commentaries can be helpful in Bible study, but wait to use commentaries until after you've observed the text and attempted interpretation using other translations, a dictionary, and cross-references, and overlaying the passage with the context. Ask God for insight as you study, and be willing to wait to hear from him. Again, resist the temptation to jump to someone else's thoughts before observing and interpreting on your own. For help choosing commentaries, begin by asking trusted leaders about their favorites.[4]

The ultimate goal of Bible study is to know and love God. So observe, interpret, apply, and enjoy God! Stay in conversation with him, asking him to help you understand the Scriptures. Ask him your hard questions. Listen to him. He wants to meet you in your study of the Bible!

WHY STUDY THE STORY OF JACOB?

We worship the God of Abraham, Isaac, and Jacob. Knowing the stories of our patriarchs and God's covenant with them helps us understand the rest of the Bible.

Jacob is a key figure in the Bible. He is mentioned in the Scriptures over three hundred times, over twenty times in the New Testament alone. Jacob's name was changed by God to Israel, and his sons gave rise to the twelve tribes of Israel. The people of Israel laid claim to the promised land based on the covenant God made with Abraham, then with Isaac and later Jacob. It was Jacob's family of seventy who journeyed to Egypt because of the famine in Canaan. It was his family who multiplied in the land of Egypt for over four hundred years, becoming so great in number that Pharaoh was afraid of them. And it was the descendants of Jacob who exited Egypt by the thousands under the leadership of Moses.

Jacob's family relationships were difficult throughout his whole life. His father-in-law deceived him and cheated him multiple times. His parents, Isaac and Rebekah, showed overt favoritism, causing tension and conflict between Jacob and his older twin brother, Esau. Jacob did not break the pattern, showing overt favoritism for one wife and one son, causing monumental tension and conflict for his entire family.

Jacob rightly represents God's people who waver between trusting God and trusting in something else. Jacob often failed to trust God's covenant and timing. He spent much of his life in conflict due to his own schemes. Although Jacob vacillated between trusting God and trusting in his own plans, God did not waver in his faithfulness to Jacob. Interestingly, authors of the Old Testament referred to this patriarch as both Israel and Jacob, often within the same verse.

The story of Jacob offers timely reminders about how to live as the people of God, trusting God's timing and faithfulness. God will always do what he says he will do. Always. Our hasty plans, deceptions, and utter failures will make life harder, but they cannot thwart the plans or inhibit the love and faithfulness of the God of Abraham, Isaac, and Jacob.

Joyfully,
COLLEEN SEARCY

GETTING STARTED IN THE STORY OF JACOB

We have our best chance of understanding the story of Jacob if we overlay the text in Genesis with important context. Below are context questions to address before you begin the study.[5] For help answering these questions, you can watch my Getting Started video at colleensearcy.com/mmibteaching.

1. Who wrote the story of Jacob, recorded in the book of Genesis?

2. When was the book of Genesis written?

3. To whom was it written and for what purpose?

4. In what style was the book of Genesis written? Turn to Tool 3 in the Tool Kit for help identifying the genre.[6]

5. What are the central themes of the book of Genesis?

6. Turn to Tool 1 in the Tool Kit. Place an *X* on the timeline to determine where the story of Jacob lands in the whole story of the Bible.

1
JACOB WRESTLES WITH ESAU

Genesis 25:19–26:35

JACOB WRESTLES WITH ESAU

Genesis 25:19–26:35

19 These are the generations of Isaac, Abraham's son: Abraham fathered
Isaac, 20 and Isaac was forty years old when he took Rebekah, the daughter
of Bethuel the Aramean of Paddan-aram, the sister of Laban the Aramean,
to be his wife. 21 And Isaac prayed to the LORD for his wife, because she was
barren. And the LORD granted his prayer, and Rebekah his wife conceived.
22 The children struggled together within her, and she said, "If it is thus,
why is this happening to me?" So she went to inquire of the LORD. 23 And
the LORD said to her,

> "Two nations are in your womb,
>   and two peoples from within you shall be divided;
> the one shall be stronger than the other,
>   the older shall serve the younger."

24 When her days to give birth were completed, behold, there were twins in
her womb. 25 The first came out red, all his body like a hairy cloak, so they
called his name Esau. 26 Afterward his brother came out with his hand holding
Esau's heel, so his name was called Jacob. Isaac was sixty years old when
she bore them.

27 When the boys grew up, Esau was a skillful hunter, a man of the field,
while Jacob was a quiet man, dwelling in tents. 28 Isaac loved Esau because
he ate of his game, but Rebekah loved Jacob.

29 Once when Jacob was cooking stew, Esau came in from the field, and he
was exhausted. 30 And Esau said to Jacob, "Let me eat some of that red stew,
for I am exhausted!" (Therefore his name was called Edom.) 31 Jacob said,
"Sell me your birthright now." 32 Esau said, "I am about to die; of what use

is a birthright to me?” 33 Jacob said, “Swear to me now.” So he swore to him
and sold his birthright to Jacob. 34 Then Jacob gave Esau bread and lentil
stew, and he ate and drank and rose and went his way. Thus Esau despised
his birthright.

26:1 Now there was a famine in the land, besides the former famine that was
in the days of Abraham. And Isaac went to Gerar to Abimelech king of the
Philistines. 2 And the LORD appeared to him and said, “Do not go down to
Egypt; dwell in the land of which I shall tell you. 3 Sojourn in this land, and
I will be with you and will bless you, for to you and to your offspring I will
give all these lands, and I will establish the oath that I swore to Abraham
your father. 4 I will multiply your offspring as the stars of heaven and will
give to your offspring all these lands. And in your offspring all the nations
of the earth shall be blessed, 5 because Abraham obeyed my voice and kept
my charge, my commandments, my statutes, and my laws.”

6 So Isaac settled in Gerar. 7 When the men of the place asked him about his
wife, he said, “She is my sister,” for he feared to say, “My wife,” thinking, “lest
the men of the place should kill me because of Rebekah,” because she was
attractive in appearance. 8 When he had been there a long time, Abimelech
king of the Philistines looked out of a window and saw Isaac laughing with
Rebekah his wife. 9 So Abimelech called Isaac and said, “Behold, she is your
wife. How then could you say, ‘She is my sister’?” Isaac said to him, “Because
I thought, ‘Lest I die because of her.’ ” 10 Abimelech said, “What is this you have
done to us? One of the people might easily have lain with your wife, and you
would have brought guilt upon us.” 11 So Abimelech warned all the people,
saying, “Whoever touches this man or his wife shall surely be put to death.”

12 And Isaac sowed in that land and reaped in the same year a hundredfold.
The LORD blessed him, 13 and the man became rich, and gained more and
more until he became very wealthy. 14 He had possessions of flocks and herds
and many servants, so that the Philistines envied him. 15 (Now the Philistines

had stopped and filled with earth all the wells that his father's servants had dug in the days of Abraham his father.) 16 And Abimelech said to Isaac, "Go away from us, for you are much mightier than we."

17 So Isaac departed from there and encamped in the Valley of Gerar and settled there. 18 And Isaac dug again the wells of water that had been dug in the days of Abraham his father, which the Philistines had stopped after the death of Abraham. And he gave them the names that his father had given them. 19 But when Isaac's servants dug in the valley and found there a well of spring water, 20 the herdsmen of Gerar quarreled with Isaac's herdsmen, saying, "The water is ours." So he called the name of the well Esek, because they contended with him. 21 Then they dug another well, and they quarreled over that also, so he called its name Sitnah. 22 And he moved from there and dug another well, and they did not quarrel over it. So he called its name Rehoboth, saying, "For now the LORD has made room for us, and we shall be fruitful in the land."

23 From there he went up to Beersheba. 24 And the LORD appeared to him the same night and said, "I am the God of Abraham your father. Fear not, for I am with you and will bless you and multiply your offspring for my servant Abraham's sake." 25 So he built an altar there and called upon the name of the LORD and pitched his tent there. And there Isaac's servants dug a well.

26 When Abimelech went to him from Gerar with Ahuzzath his adviser and Phicol the commander of his army, 27 Isaac said to them, "Why have you come to me, seeing that you hate me and have sent me away from you?" 28 They said, "We see plainly that the LORD has been with you. So we said, let there be a sworn pact between us, between you and us, and let us make a covenant with you, 29 that you will do us no harm, just as we have not touched you and have done to you nothing but good and have sent you away in peace. You are now the blessed of the LORD." 30 So he made them a feast, and they ate and drank. 31 In the morning they rose early and exchanged oaths.

And Isaac sent them on their way, and they departed from him in peace.
32 That same day Isaac's servants came and told him about the well that
they had dug and said to him, "We have found water." 33 He called it Shibah;
therefore the name of the city is Beersheba to this day.

34 When Esau was forty years old, he took Judith the daughter of Beeri the
Hittite to be his wife, and Basemath the daughter of Elon the Hittite, 35 and
they made life bitter for Isaac and Rebekah.

NOTES

OBSERVE: WHAT DOES THE PASSAGE SAY?

Step 1: Setting and Summary

Key Characters and Locations

CHARACTERS:

- *Isaac.* Son of Abraham and Sarah; husband of Rebekah, father of Esau and Jacob.
- *Rebekah.* Wife of Isaac; sister of Laban. She was barren but conceived twin boys because the Lord granted Isaac's prayer for her.
- *Esau.* Firstborn of Isaac and Rebekah and Jacob's twin.
- *Jacob.* Younger son of Isaac and Rebekah and Esau's twin.
- *Abimelech.* King of the Philistines; possibly same man in Genesis 20 with Abraham (and same deception!) or perhaps his descendant.

LOCATIONS:

See if you can find these locations on the map in Tool 2 of the Tool Kit.

- *Gerar.* Inhabited by Philistines; where Isaac sojourned during the famine in Canaan. In contrast to his father, Abraham, Isaac listened to the Lord and did not go to Egypt.
- *Beersheba.* Where Isaac moved after Gerar. God appeared to Isaac in Beersheba and promised to be with him, bless him, and multiply his offspring; restating the covenant given to his father, Abraham.

Summary of the Passage

What Stood Out to You or Piqued Your Curiosity?

Step 2: Key Words and Phrases

Remember to look at the prompts on your Bible study bookmark as you observe the text.

- *Twos*: two nations in Rebekah's womb; "two peoples from within you"; twins (Isaac loved one, Rebekah loved the other).
- *Birthright*: 4 times!
- *"And the Lord appeared"*: 2 times!
- *Wells.* Wells are mentioned a lot.

Remember to enjoy God and listen as you study. Move to a time of prayer after you observe, recording your prayer on the prayer pages in Tool 6.

NOTES

INTERPRET: WHAT DOES THE PASSAGE MEAN?

Step 3: What Was Hard to Understand?

Questions

- *What does it mean that Esau despised his birthright?*
- *Why did God bless Isaac after he handed over Rebekah to Abimelech?*
- *Why are the wells mentioned so many times? What is the significance?*

Insights from Cross-References, Other Translations, and the Context

Remember that historical context is one of the greatest Bible study tools available. Keep asking the questions: Who wrote this? When did he write it? Where does this land in the whole story of the Bible? How would these words land on the ears of the original hearers?

- *What does it mean that Esau despised his birthright?* Genesis 25:32 in the New Living Translation reads: "Look, I'm dying of starvation!" said Esau. And, "What good is my birthright to me now?" In the cross-reference Hebrews 12:16, we read that Esau was unholy for selling his birthright for a meal—a temporary craving. He treated the covenant blessing linked to firstborn status as trivial.
- *Why did God bless Isaac after he handed over Rebekah to Abimelech?* Hint: Look back at the context on page 13 to gain insight. Who wrote the book of Genesis? To whom was he writing? Where had they just come from? How might both the stories of Abraham in Gerar (Genesis 20) and Isaac in Gerar strengthen the faith of the original hearers? Also, remember that authors of historical narrative recorded what actually happened, not what should have happened.
- *Why are the wells mentioned so many times? What is the significance?* Hint: Think back to the context. Who were the original hearers? How might they be encouraged by the story of Isaac redigging the wells of Abraham in the land of Canaan?

Remember to turn to the Questions for Further Thought and Discussion in Tool 7 for a deeper dive. Additional historical context is also given within the questions.

Step 4: What Did You Learn about God?

Refer to the attributes of God in Tool 4 if needed.

Remember to enjoy God and listen as you study. Move to a time of prayer after you interpret, recording your prayer on the prayer pages in Tool 6.

NOTES

APPLY: HOW WILL YOU APPLY THE PASSAGE?

Step 5: What Did You Learn about People?

Others

Remember to look at the prompts on your Bible study bookmark as you apply the text.

Yourself

- *Is there a command to obey? An example to follow? A sin to confess? A warning to heed? An encouragement to receive?*
- *What action step will you take?*

Wrap Up: What Did You Discover in the Scriptures That Was Important to You?

Remember to enjoy God and listen as you study. Move to a time of prayer after you apply, recording your prayer on the prayer pages in Tool 6.

2
JACOB DECEIVES, GOD PROMISES

Genesis 27:1–28:22

JACOB DECEIVES, GOD PROMISES

Genesis 27:1–28:22

1 When Isaac was old and his eyes were dim so that he could not see, he called Esau his older son and said to him, "My son"; and he answered, "Here I am." 2 He said, "Behold, I am old; I do not know the day of my death. 3 Now then, take your weapons, your quiver and your bow, and go out to the field and hunt game for me, 4 and prepare for me delicious food, such as I love, and bring it to me so that I may eat, that my soul may bless you before I die."

5 Now Rebekah was listening when Isaac spoke to his son Esau. So when Esau went to the field to hunt for game and bring it, 6 Rebekah said to her son Jacob, "I heard your father speak to your brother Esau, 7 'Bring me game and prepare for me delicious food, that I may eat it and bless you before the LORD before I die.' 8 Now therefore, my son, obey my voice as I command you. 9 Go to the flock and bring me two good young goats, so that I may prepare from them delicious food for your father, such as he loves. 10 And you shall bring it to your father to eat, so that he may bless you before he dies." 11 But Jacob said to Rebekah his mother, "Behold, my brother Esau is a hairy man, and I am a smooth man. 12 Perhaps my father will feel me, and I shall seem to be mocking him and bring a curse upon myself and not a blessing." 13 His mother said to him, "Let your curse be on me, my son; only obey my voice, and go, bring them to me."

14 So he went and took them and brought them to his mother, and his mother prepared delicious food, such as his father loved. 15 Then Rebekah took the best garments of Esau her older son, which were with her in the house, and put them on Jacob her younger son. 16 And the skins of the young goats she put on his hands and on the smooth part of his neck. 17 And she put the delicious food and the bread, which she had prepared, into the hand of her son Jacob.

18 So he went in to his father and said, "My father." And he said, "Here I am. Who are you, my son?" 19 Jacob said to his father, "I am Esau your firstborn.

I have done as you told me; now sit up and eat of my game, that your soul
may bless me." [20] But Isaac said to his son, "How is it that you have found it
so quickly, my son?" He answered, "Because the LORD your God granted me
success." [21] Then Isaac said to Jacob, "Please come near, that I may feel you,
my son, to know whether you are really my son Esau or not." [22] So Jacob went
near to Isaac his father, who felt him and said, "The voice is Jacob's voice, but
the hands are the hands of Esau." [23] And he did not recognize him, because
his hands were hairy like his brother Esau's hands. So he blessed him. [24] He
said, "Are you really my son Esau?" He answered, "I am." [25] Then he said,
"Bring it near to me, that I may eat of my son's game and bless you." So he
brought it near to him, and he ate; and he brought him wine, and he drank.
[26] Then his father Isaac said to him, "Come near and kiss me, my son." [27] So
he came near and kissed him. And Isaac smelled the smell of his garments
and blessed him and said,

"See, the smell of my son
  is as the smell of a field that the LORD has blessed!
28 May God give you of the dew of heaven
  and of the fatness of the earth
  and plenty of grain and wine.
29 Let peoples serve you,
  and nations bow down to you.
Be lord over your brothers,
  and may your mother's sons bow down to you.
Cursed be everyone who curses you,
  and blessed be everyone who blesses you!"

[30] As soon as Isaac had finished blessing Jacob, when Jacob had scarcely
gone out from the presence of Isaac his father, Esau his brother came in from

his hunting. [31] He also prepared delicious food and brought it to his father.
And he said to his father, "Let my father arise and eat of his son's game,
that you may bless me." [32] His father Isaac said to him, "Who are you?" He
answered, "I am your son, your firstborn, Esau." [33] Then Isaac trembled very
violently and said, "Who was it then that hunted game and brought it to me,
and I ate it all before you came, and I have blessed him? Yes, and he shall be
blessed." [34] As soon as Esau heard the words of his father, he cried out with
an exceedingly great and bitter cry and said to his father, "Bless me, even me
also, O my father!" [35] But he said, "Your brother came deceitfully, and he has
taken away your blessing." [36] Esau said, "Is he not rightly named Jacob? For
he has cheated me these two times. He took away my birthright, and behold,
now he has taken away my blessing." Then he said, "Have you not reserved
a blessing for me?" [37] Isaac answered and said to Esau, "Behold, I have made
him lord over you, and all his brothers I have given to him for servants, and
with grain and wine I have sustained him. What then can I do for you, my
son?" [38] Esau said to his father, "Have you but one blessing, my father? Bless
me, even me also, O my father." And Esau lifted up his voice and wept.

[39] Then Isaac his father answered and said to him:

"Behold, away from the fatness of the earth shall your dwelling be,
and away from the dew of heaven on high.
40 By your sword you shall live,
and you shall serve your brother;
but when you grow restless
you shall break his yoke from your neck."

[41] Now Esau hated Jacob because of the blessing with which his father had
blessed him, and Esau said to himself, "The days of mourning for my father
are approaching; then I will kill my brother Jacob." [42] But the words of Esau

her older son were told to Rebekah. So she sent and called Jacob her younger
son and said to him, "Behold, your brother Esau comforts himself about you
by planning to kill you. 43 Now therefore, my son, obey my voice. Arise, flee to
Laban my brother in Haran 44 and stay with him a while, until your brother's
fury turns away— 45 until your brother's anger turns away from you, and he
forgets what you have done to him. Then I will send and bring you from
there. Why should I be bereft of you both in one day?"

46 Then Rebekah said to Isaac, "I loathe my life because of the Hittite
women. If Jacob marries one of the Hittite women like these, one of the
women of the land, what good will my life be to me?"

28:1 Then Isaac called Jacob and blessed him and directed him, "You must
not take a wife from the Canaanite women. 2 Arise, go to Paddan-aram to the
house of Bethuel your mother's father, and take as your wife from there one
of the daughters of Laban your mother's brother. 3 God Almighty bless you
and make you fruitful and multiply you, that you may become a company of
peoples. 4 May he give the blessing of Abraham to you and to your offspring
with you, that you may take possession of the land of your sojournings that
God gave to Abraham!" 5 Thus Isaac sent Jacob away. And he went to Paddan-aram, to Laban, the son of Bethuel the Aramean, the brother of Rebekah,
Jacob's and Esau's mother.

6 Now Esau saw that Isaac had blessed Jacob and sent him away to Paddan-aram to take a wife from there, and that as he blessed him he directed
him, "You must not take a wife from the Canaanite women," 7 and that Jacob
had obeyed his father and his mother and gone to Paddan-aram. 8 So when
Esau saw that the Canaanite women did not please Isaac his father, 9 Esau
went to Ishmael and took as his wife, besides the wives he had, Mahalath the
daughter of Ishmael, Abraham's son, the sister of Nebaioth.

10 Jacob left Beersheba and went toward Haran. 11 And he came to a certain
place and stayed there that night, because the sun had set. Taking one of the

stones of the place, he put it under his head and lay down in that place to
sleep. [12] And he dreamed, and behold, there was a ladder set up on the earth,
and the top of it reached to heaven. And behold, the angels of God were
ascending and descending on it! [13] And behold, the LORD stood above it and
said, "I am the LORD, the God of Abraham your father and the God of Isaac.
The land on which you lie I will give to you and to your offspring. [14] Your offspring shall be like the dust of the earth, and you shall spread abroad to the
west and to the east and to the north and to the south, and in you and your
offspring shall all the families of the earth be blessed. [15] Behold, I am with
you and will keep you wherever you go, and will bring you back to this land.
For I will not leave you until I have done what I have promised you." [16] Then
Jacob awoke from his sleep and said, "Surely the LORD is in this place, and
I did not know it." [17] And he was afraid and said, "How awesome is this place!
This is none other than the house of God, and this is the gate of heaven."

[18] So early in the morning Jacob took the stone that he had put under his
head and set it up for a pillar and poured oil on the top of it. [19] He called the
name of that place Bethel, but the name of the city was Luz at the first. [20] Then
Jacob made a vow, saying, "If God will be with me and will keep me in this
way that I go, and will give me bread to eat and clothing to wear, [21] so that
I come again to my father's house in peace, then the LORD shall be my God,
[22] and this stone, which I have set up for a pillar, shall be God's house. And
of all that you give me I will give a full tenth to you."

OBSERVE: WHAT DOES THE PASSAGE SAY?

Step 1: Setting and Summary

Key Characters and Locations

CHARACTERS:

LOCATIONS:

Summary of the Passage

What Stood Out to You or Piqued Your Curiosity?

Step 2: Key Words and Phrases

NOTES

INTERPRET: WHAT DOES THE PASSAGE MEAN?

Step 3: What Was Hard to Understand?

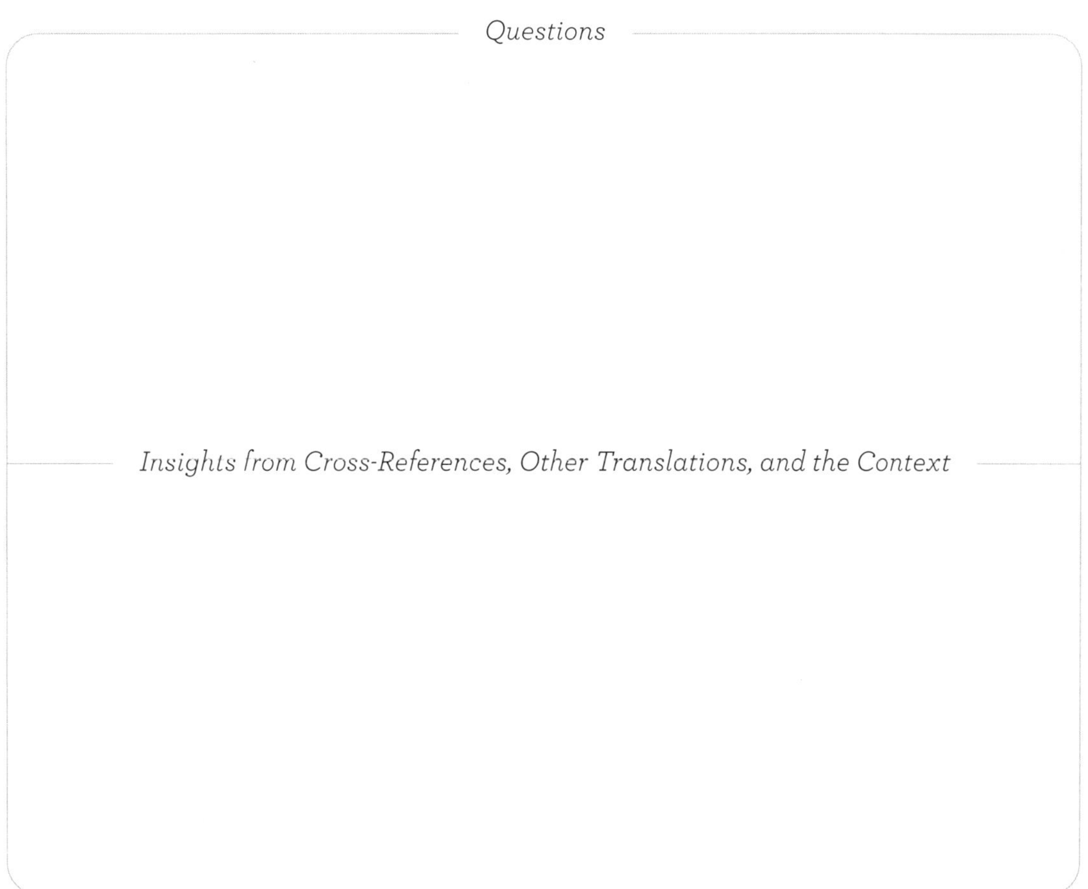

Step 4: What Did You Learn about God?

Refer to the attributes of God in Tool 4 if needed.

NOTES

APPLY: HOW WILL YOU APPLY THE PASSAGE?

Step 5: What Did You Learn about People?

Others

Yourself

Wrap Up: What Did You Discover in the Scriptures That Was Important to You?

3

JACOB, LEAH, AND RACHEL

Genesis 29:1–30:24

JACOB, LEAH, AND RACHEL

Genesis 29:1–30:24

[1]Then Jacob went on his journey and came to the land of the people of the east. [2]As he looked, he saw a well in the field, and behold, three flocks of sheep lying beside it, for out of that well the flocks were watered. The stone on the well's mouth was large, [3]and when all the flocks were gathered there, the shepherds would roll the stone from the mouth of the well and water the sheep, and put the stone back in its place over the mouth of the well.

[4]Jacob said to them, "My brothers, where do you come from?" They said, "We are from Haran." [5]He said to them, "Do you know Laban the son of Nahor?" They said, "We know him." [6]He said to them, "Is it well with him?" They said, "It is well; and see, Rachel his daughter is coming with the sheep!" [7]He said, "Behold, it is still high day; it is not time for the livestock to be gathered together. Water the sheep and go, pasture them." [8]But they said, "We cannot until all the flocks are gathered together and the stone is rolled from the mouth of the well; then we water the sheep."

[9]While he was still speaking with them, Rachel came with her father's sheep, for she was a shepherdess. [10]Now as soon as Jacob saw Rachel the daughter of Laban his mother's brother, and the sheep of Laban his mother's brother, Jacob came near and rolled the stone from the well's mouth and watered the flock of Laban his mother's brother. [11]Then Jacob kissed Rachel and wept aloud. [12]And Jacob told Rachel that he was her father's kinsman, and that he was Rebekah's son, and she ran and told her father.

[13]As soon as Laban heard the news about Jacob, his sister's son, he ran to meet him and embraced him and kissed him and brought him to his house. Jacob told Laban all these things, [14]and Laban said to him, "Surely you are my bone and my flesh!" And he stayed with him a month.

15 Then Laban said to Jacob, "Because you are my kinsman, should you
therefore serve me for nothing? Tell me, what shall your wages be?" 16 Now
Laban had two daughters. The name of the older was Leah, and the name of
the younger was Rachel. 17 Leah's eyes were weak, but Rachel was beautiful
in form and appearance. 18 Jacob loved Rachel. And he said, "I will serve you
seven years for your younger daughter Rachel." 19 Laban said, "It is better
that I give her to you than that I should give her to any other man; stay with
me." 20 So Jacob served seven years for Rachel, and they seemed to him but
a few days because of the love he had for her.

21 Then Jacob said to Laban, "Give me my wife that I may go in to her, for
my time is completed." 22 So Laban gathered together all the people of the
place and made a feast. 23 But in the evening he took his daughter Leah and
brought her to Jacob, and he went in to her. 24 (Laban gave his female servant Zilpah to his daughter Leah to be her servant.) 25 And in the morning,
behold, it was Leah! And Jacob said to Laban, "What is this you have done
to me? Did I not serve with you for Rachel? Why then have you deceived
me?" 26 Laban said, "It is not so done in our country, to give the younger
before the firstborn. 27 Complete the week of this one, and we will give you
the other also in return for serving me another seven years." 28 Jacob did so,
and completed her week. Then Laban gave him his daughter Rachel to be
his wife. 29 (Laban gave his female servant Bilhah to his daughter Rachel to
be her servant.) 30 So Jacob went in to Rachel also, and he loved Rachel more
than Leah, and served Laban for another seven years.

31 When the LORD saw that Leah was hated, he opened her womb, but Rachel
was barren. 32 And Leah conceived and bore a son, and she called his name
Reuben, for she said, "Because the LORD has looked upon my affliction; for
now my husband will love me." 33 She conceived again and bore a son, and
said, "Because the LORD has heard that I am hated, he has given me this
son also." And she called his name Simeon. 34 Again she conceived and bore

a son, and said, "Now this time my husband will be attached to me, because I have borne him three sons." Therefore his name was called Levi. 35 And she conceived again and bore a son, and said, "This time I will praise the LORD." Therefore she called his name Judah. Then she ceased bearing.

30:1 When Rachel saw that she bore Jacob no children, she envied her sister. She said to Jacob, "Give me children, or I shall die!" 2 Jacob's anger was kindled against Rachel, and he said, "Am I in the place of God, who has withheld from you the fruit of the womb?" 3 Then she said, "Here is my servant Bilhah; go in to her, so that she may give birth on my behalf, that even I may have children through her." 4 So she gave him her servant Bilhah as a wife, and Jacob went in to her. 5 And Bilhah conceived and bore Jacob a son. 6 Then Rachel said, "God has judged me, and has also heard my voice and given me a son." Therefore she called his name Dan. 7 Rachel's servant Bilhah conceived again and bore Jacob a second son. 8 Then Rachel said, "With mighty wrestlings I have wrestled with my sister and have prevailed." So she called his name Naphtali.

9 When Leah saw that she had ceased bearing children, she took her servant Zilpah and gave her to Jacob as a wife. 10 Then Leah's servant Zilpah bore Jacob a son. 11 And Leah said, "Good fortune has come!" so she called his name Gad. 12 Leah's servant Zilpah bore Jacob a second son. 13 And Leah said, "Happy am I! For women have called me happy." So she called his name Asher.

14 In the days of wheat harvest Reuben went and found mandrakes in the field and brought them to his mother Leah. Then Rachel said to Leah, "Please give me some of your son's mandrakes." 15 But she said to her, "Is it a small matter that you have taken away my husband? Would you take away my son's mandrakes also?" Rachel said, "Then he may lie with you tonight in exchange for your son's mandrakes." 16 When Jacob came from the field in the evening, Leah went out to meet him and said, "You must come in to

me, for I have hired you with my son's mandrakes." So he lay with her that
night. 17 And God listened to Leah, and she conceived and bore Jacob a fifth
son. 18 Leah said, "God has given me my wages because I gave my servant
to my husband." So she called his name Issachar.

19 And Leah conceived again, and she bore Jacob a sixth son. 20 Then Leah
said, "God has endowed me with a good endowment; now my husband
will honor me, because I have borne him six sons." So she called his name
Zebulun. 21 Afterward she bore a daughter and called her name Dinah.

22 Then God remembered Rachel, and God listened to her and opened her
womb. 23 She conceived and bore a son and said, "God has taken away my
reproach." 24 And she called his name Joseph, saying, "May the LORD add to
me another son!"

NOTES

OBSERVE: WHAT DOES THE PASSAGE SAY?

Step 1: Setting and Summary

Key Characters and Locations

CHARACTERS:

LOCATIONS:

Summary of the Passage

What Stood Out to You or Piqued Your Curiosity?

Step 2: Key Words and Phrases

NOTES

INTERPRET: WHAT DOES THE PASSAGE MEAN?

Step 3: What Was Hard to Understand?

Questions

Insights from Cross-References, Other Translations, and the Context

Step 4: What Did You Learn about God?

Refer to the attributes of God in Tool 4 if needed.

NOTES

APPLY: HOW WILL YOU APPLY THE PASSAGE?

Step 5: What Did You Learn about People?

Others

Yourself

Wrap Up: What Did You Discover in the Scriptures That Was Important to You?

4

JACOB WRESTLES WITH LABAN

Genesis 30:25–31:55

JACOB WRESTLES WITH LABAN

Genesis 30:25–31:55

25 As soon as Rachel had borne Joseph, Jacob said to Laban, "Send me away, that I may go to my own home and country. 26 Give me my wives and my children for whom I have served you, that I may go, for you know the service that I have given you." 27 But Laban said to him, "If I have found favor in your sight, I have learned by divination that the LORD has blessed me because of you. 28 Name your wages, and I will give it." 29 Jacob said to him, "You yourself know how I have served you, and how your livestock has fared with me. 30 For you had little before I came, and it has increased abundantly, and the LORD has blessed you wherever I turned. But now when shall I provide for my own household also?" 31 He said, "What shall I give you?" Jacob said, "You shall not give me anything. If you will do this for me, I will again pasture your flock and keep it: 32 let me pass through all your flock today, removing from it every speckled and spotted sheep and every black lamb, and the spotted and speckled among the goats, and they shall be my wages. 33 So my honesty will answer for me later, when you come to look into my wages with you. Every one that is not speckled and spotted among the goats and black among the lambs, if found with me, shall be counted stolen." 34 Laban said, "Good! Let it be as you have said." 35 But that day Laban removed the male goats that were striped and spotted, and all the female goats that were speckled and spotted, every one that had white on it, and every lamb that was black, and put them in the charge of his sons. 36 And he set a distance of three days' journey between himself and Jacob, and Jacob pastured the rest of Laban's flock.

37 Then Jacob took fresh sticks of poplar and almond and plane trees, and peeled white streaks in them, exposing the white of the sticks. 38 He set the sticks that he had peeled in front of the flocks in the troughs, that is, the

watering places, where the flocks came to drink. And since they bred when
they came to drink, [39] the flocks bred in front of the sticks and so the flocks
brought forth striped, speckled, and spotted. [40] And Jacob separated the
lambs and set the faces of the flocks toward the striped and all the black in
the flock of Laban. He put his own droves apart and did not put them with
Laban's flock. [41] Whenever the stronger of the flock were breeding, Jacob
would lay the sticks in the troughs before the eyes of the flock, that they
might breed among the sticks, [42] but for the feebler of the flock he would not
lay them there. So the feebler would be Laban's, and the stronger Jacob's.
[43] Thus the man increased greatly and had large flocks, female servants and
male servants, and camels and donkeys.

[31:1] Now Jacob heard that the sons of Laban were saying, "Jacob has taken
all that was our father's, and from what was our father's he has gained all
this wealth." [2] And Jacob saw that Laban did not regard him with favor as
before. [3] Then the LORD said to Jacob, "Return to the land of your fathers
and to your kindred, and I will be with you."

[4] So Jacob sent and called Rachel and Leah into the field where his flock
was [5] and said to them, "I see that your father does not regard me with favor
as he did before. But the God of my father has been with me. [6] You know that
I have served your father with all my strength, [7] yet your father has cheated
me and changed my wages ten times. But God did not permit him to harm
me. [8] If he said, 'The spotted shall be your wages,' then all the flock bore
spotted; and if he said, 'The striped shall be your wages,' then all the flock
bore striped. [9] Thus God has taken away the livestock of your father and given
them to me. [10] In the breeding season of the flock I lifted up my eyes and saw
in a dream that the goats that mated with the flock were striped, spotted, and
mottled. [11] Then the angel of God said to me in the dream, 'Jacob,' and I said,
'Here I am!' [12] And he said, 'Lift up your eyes and see, all the goats that mate
with the flock are striped, spotted, and mottled, for I have seen all that Laban is

doing to you. 13 I am the God of Bethel, where you anointed a pillar and made
a vow to me. Now arise, go out from this land and return to the land of your
kindred.'" 14 Then Rachel and Leah answered and said to him, "Is there any
portion or inheritance left to us in our father's house? 15 Are we not regarded
by him as foreigners? For he has sold us, and he has indeed devoured our
money. 16 All the wealth that God has taken away from our father belongs to
us and to our children. Now then, whatever God has said to you, do."

17 So Jacob arose and set his sons and his wives on camels. 18 He drove
away all his livestock, all his property that he had gained, the livestock in his
possession that he had acquired in Paddan-aram, to go to the land of Canaan
to his father Isaac. 19 Laban had gone to shear his sheep, and Rachel stole her
father's household gods. 20 And Jacob tricked Laban the Aramean, by not
telling him that he intended to flee. 21 He fled with all that he had and arose
and crossed the Euphrates, and set his face toward the hill country of Gilead.

22 When it was told Laban on the third day that Jacob had fled, 23 he took his
kinsmen with him and pursued him for seven days and followed close after
him into the hill country of Gilead. 24 But God came to Laban the Aramean in
a dream by night and said to him, "Be careful not to say anything to Jacob,
either good or bad."

25 And Laban overtook Jacob. Now Jacob had pitched his tent in the hill
country, and Laban with his kinsmen pitched tents in the hill country of
Gilead. 26 And Laban said to Jacob, "What have you done, that you have
tricked me and driven away my daughters like captives of the sword? 27 Why
did you flee secretly and trick me, and did not tell me, so that I might have
sent you away with mirth and songs, with tambourine and lyre? 28 And why did
you not permit me to kiss my sons and my daughters farewell? Now you have
done foolishly. 29 It is in my power to do you harm. But the God of your father
spoke to me last night, saying, 'Be careful not to say anything to Jacob, either
good or bad.' 30 And now you have gone away because you longed greatly

for your father's house, but why did you steal my gods?" [31] Jacob answered
and said to Laban, "Because I was afraid, for I thought that you would take
your daughters from me by force. [32] Anyone with whom you find your gods
shall not live. In the presence of our kinsmen point out what I have that is
yours, and take it." Now Jacob did not know that Rachel had stolen them.

[33] So Laban went into Jacob's tent and into Leah's tent and into the tent of
the two female servants, but he did not find them. And he went out of Leah's
tent and entered Rachel's. [34] Now Rachel had taken the household gods and
put them in the camel's saddle and sat on them. Laban felt all about the
tent, but did not find them. [35] And she said to her father, "Let not my lord be
angry that I cannot rise before you, for the way of women is upon me." So
he searched but did not find the household gods.

[36] Then Jacob became angry and berated Laban. Jacob said to Laban,
"What is my offense? What is my sin, that you have hotly pursued me? [37] For
you have felt through all my goods; what have you found of all your household goods? Set it here before my kinsmen and your kinsmen, that they may
decide between us two. [38] These twenty years I have been with you. Your
ewes and your female goats have not miscarried, and I have not eaten the
rams of your flocks. [39] What was torn by wild beasts I did not bring to you.
I bore the loss of it myself. From my hand you required it, whether stolen by
day or stolen by night. [40] There I was: by day the heat consumed me, and the
cold by night, and my sleep fled from my eyes. [41] These twenty years I have
been in your house. I served you fourteen years for your two daughters, and
six years for your flock, and you have changed my wages ten times. [42] If the
God of my father, the God of Abraham and the Fear of Isaac, had not been
on my side, surely now you would have sent me away empty-handed. God
saw my affliction and the labor of my hands and rebuked you last night."

[43] Then Laban answered and said to Jacob, "The daughters are my daughters, the children are my children, the flocks are my flocks, and all that you

see is mine. But what can I do this day for these my daughters or for their
children whom they have borne? 44 Come now, let us make a covenant,
you and I. And let it be a witness between you and me." 45 So Jacob took
a stone and set it up as a pillar. 46 And Jacob said to his kinsmen, "Gather
stones." And they took stones and made a heap, and they ate there by the
heap. 47 Laban called it Jegar-sahadutha, but Jacob called it Galeed. 48 Laban
said, "This heap is a witness between you and me today." Therefore he named
it Galeed, 49 and Mizpah, for he said, "The LORD watch between you and me,
when we are out of one another's sight. 50 If you oppress my daughters, or if
you take wives besides my daughters, although no one is with us, see, God
is witness between you and me."

51 Then Laban said to Jacob, "See this heap and the pillar, which I have set
between you and me. 52 This heap is a witness, and the pillar is a witness, that
I will not pass over this heap to you, and you will not pass over this heap and
this pillar to me, to do harm. 53 The God of Abraham and the God of Nahor,
the God of their father, judge between us." So Jacob swore by the Fear of his
father Isaac, 54 and Jacob offered a sacrifice in the hill country and called his
kinsmen to eat bread. They ate bread and spent the night in the hill country.

55 Early in the morning Laban arose and kissed his grandchildren and
his daughters and blessed them. Then Laban departed and returned home.

OBSERVE: WHAT DOES THE PASSAGE SAY?

Step 1: Setting and Summary

Key Characters and Locations

CHARACTERS:

LOCATIONS:

Summary of the Passage

What Stood Out to You or Piqued Your Curiosity?

Step 2: Key Words and Phrases

NOTES

INTERPRET: WHAT DOES THE PASSAGE MEAN?

Step 3: What Was Hard to Understand?

Questions

Insights from Cross-References, Other Translations, and the Context

Step 4: What Did You Learn about God?

Refer to the attributes of God in Tool 4 if needed.

NOTES

APPLY: HOW WILL YOU APPLY THE PASSAGE?

Step 5: What Did You Learn about People?

Others

Yourself

Wrap Up: What Did You Discover in the Scriptures That Was Important to You?

5
JACOB WRESTLES WITH GOD

Genesis 32:1–33:20

JACOB WRESTLES WITH GOD

Genesis 32:1–33:20

1 Jacob went on his way, and the angels of God met him. 2 And when Jacob
saw them he said, "This is God's camp!" So he called the name of that place
Mahanaim.

3 And Jacob sent messengers before him to Esau his brother in the land of
Seir, the country of Edom, 4 instructing them, "Thus you shall say to my lord
Esau: Thus says your servant Jacob, 'I have sojourned with Laban and stayed
until now. 5 I have oxen, donkeys, flocks, male servants, and female servants.
I have sent to tell my lord, in order that I may find favor in your sight.'"

6 And the messengers returned to Jacob, saying, "We came to your brother
Esau, and he is coming to meet you, and there are four hundred men with
him." 7 Then Jacob was greatly afraid and distressed. He divided the people
who were with him, and the flocks and herds and camels, into two camps,
8 thinking, "If Esau comes to the one camp and attacks it, then the camp that
is left will escape."

9 And Jacob said, "O God of my father Abraham and God of my father
Isaac, O LORD who said to me, 'Return to your country and to your kindred,
that I may do you good,' 10 I am not worthy of the least of all the deeds of
steadfast love and all the faithfulness that you have shown to your servant,
for with only my staff I crossed this Jordan, and now I have become two
camps. 11 Please deliver me from the hand of my brother, from the hand of
Esau, for I fear him, that he may come and attack me, the mothers with the
children. 12 But you said, 'I will surely do you good, and make your offspring
as the sand of the sea, which cannot be numbered for multitude.'"

13 So he stayed there that night, and from what he had with him he took a
present for his brother Esau, 14 two hundred female goats and twenty male goats,
two hundred ewes and twenty rams, 15 thirty milking camels and their calves,

forty cows and ten bulls, twenty female donkeys and ten male donkeys. 16 These
he handed over to his servants, every drove by itself, and said to his servants,
"Pass on ahead of me and put a space between drove and drove." 17 He instructed
the first, "When Esau my brother meets you and asks you, 'To whom do you
belong? Where are you going? And whose are these ahead of you?' 18 then you
shall say, 'They belong to your servant Jacob. They are a present sent to my
lord Esau. And moreover, he is behind us.'" 19 He likewise instructed the second
and the third and all who followed the droves, "You shall say the same thing to
Esau when you find him, 20 and you shall say, 'Moreover, your servant Jacob is
behind us.'" For he thought, "I may appease him with the present that goes ahead
of me, and afterward I shall see his face. Perhaps he will accept me." 21 So the
present passed on ahead of him, and he himself stayed that night in the camp.

22 The same night he arose and took his two wives, his two female servants,
and his eleven children, and crossed the ford of the Jabbok. 23 He took them
and sent them across the stream, and everything else that he had. 24 And
Jacob was left alone. And a man wrestled with him until the breaking of the
day. 25 When the man saw that he did not prevail against Jacob, he touched
his hip socket, and Jacob's hip was put out of joint as he wrestled with him.
26 Then he said, "Let me go, for the day has broken." But Jacob said, "I will
not let you go unless you bless me." 27 And he said to him, "What is your
name?" And he said, "Jacob." 28 Then he said, "Your name shall no longer be
called Jacob, but Israel, for you have striven with God and with men, and
have prevailed." 29 Then Jacob asked him, "Please tell me your name." But
he said, "Why is it that you ask my name?" And there he blessed him. 30 So
Jacob called the name of the place Peniel, saying, "For I have seen God face
to face, and yet my life has been delivered." 31 The sun rose upon him as he
passed Penuel, limping because of his hip. 32 Therefore to this day the people
of Israel do not eat the sinew of the thigh that is on the hip socket, because
he touched the socket of Jacob's hip on the sinew of the thigh.

33:1 And Jacob lifted up his eyes and looked, and behold, Esau was coming,
and four hundred men with him. So he divided the children among Leah
and Rachel and the two female servants. 2 And he put the servants with their
children in front, then Leah with her children, and Rachel and Joseph last of
all. 3 He himself went on before them, bowing himself to the ground seven
times, until he came near to his brother.

4 But Esau ran to meet him and embraced him and fell on his neck and
kissed him, and they wept. 5 And when Esau lifted up his eyes and saw the
women and children, he said, "Who are these with you?" Jacob said, "The
children whom God has graciously given your servant." 6 Then the servants
drew near, they and their children, and bowed down. 7 Leah likewise and her
children drew near and bowed down. And last Joseph and Rachel drew near,
and they bowed down. 8 Esau said, "What do you mean by all this company
that I met?" Jacob answered, "To find favor in the sight of my lord." 9 But Esau
said, "I have enough, my brother; keep what you have for yourself." 10 Jacob
said, "No, please, if I have found favor in your sight, then accept my present
from my hand. For I have seen your face, which is like seeing the face of God,
and you have accepted me. 11 Please accept my blessing that is brought to
you, because God has dealt graciously with me, and because I have enough."
Thus he urged him, and he took it.

12 Then Esau said, "Let us journey on our way, and I will go ahead of you."
13 But Jacob said to him, "My lord knows that the children are frail, and that
the nursing flocks and herds are a care to me. If they are driven hard for one
day, all the flocks will die. 14 Let my lord pass on ahead of his servant, and
I will lead on slowly, at the pace of the livestock that are ahead of me and at
the pace of the children, until I come to my lord in Seir."

15 So Esau said, "Let me leave with you some of the people who are with
me." But he said, "What need is there? Let me find favor in the sight of my
lord." 16 So Esau returned that day on his way to Seir. 17 But Jacob journeyed

to Succoth, and built himself a house and made booths for his livestock. Therefore the name of the place is called Succoth.

18 And Jacob came safely to the city of Shechem, which is in the land of
Canaan, on his way from Paddan-aram, and he camped before the city. 19 And
from the sons of Hamor, Shechem's father, he bought for a hundred pieces of
money the piece of land on which he had pitched his tent. 20 There he erected
an altar and called it El-Elohe-Israel.

NOTES

OBSERVE: WHAT DOES THE PASSAGE SAY?

Step 1: Setting and Summary

Key Characters and Locations

CHARACTERS:

LOCATIONS:

Summary of the Passage

What Stood Out to You or Piqued Your Curiosity?

Step 2: Key Words and Phrases

NOTES

INTERPRET: WHAT DOES THE PASSAGE MEAN?

Step 3: What Was Hard to Understand?

Questions

Insights from Cross-References, Other Translations, and the Context

Step 4: What Did You Learn about God?

Refer to the attributes of God in Tool 4 if needed.

NOTES

APPLY: HOW WILL YOU APPLY THE PASSAGE?

Step 5: What Did You Learn about People?

Others

Yourself

Wrap Up: What Did You Discover in the Scriptures That Was Important to You?

6

THE TRAGEDY OF DINAH AND A NAME CHANGE FOR JACOB

Genesis 34:1–35:29

THE TRAGEDY OF DINAH AND A NAME CHANGE FOR JACOB

Genesis 34:1–35:29

1 Now Dinah the daughter of Leah, whom she had borne to Jacob, went out
to see the women of the land. 2 And when Shechem the son of Hamor the
Hivite, the prince of the land, saw her, he seized her and lay with her and
humiliated her. 3 And his soul was drawn to Dinah the daughter of Jacob.
He loved the young woman and spoke tenderly to her. 4 So Shechem spoke
to his father Hamor, saying, "Get me this girl for my wife."

5 Now Jacob heard that he had defiled his daughter Dinah. But his sons were
with his livestock in the field, so Jacob held his peace until they came. 6 And
Hamor the father of Shechem went out to Jacob to speak with him. 7 The sons
of Jacob had come in from the field as soon as they heard of it, and the men
were indignant and very angry, because he had done an outrageous thing
in Israel by lying with Jacob's daughter, for such a thing must not be done.

8 But Hamor spoke with them, saying, "The soul of my son Shechem longs
for your daughter. Please give her to him to be his wife. 9 Make marriages with
us. Give your daughters to us, and take our daughters for yourselves. 10 You
shall dwell with us, and the land shall be open to you. Dwell and trade in it,
and get property in it." 11 Shechem also said to her father and to her brothers,
"Let me find favor in your eyes, and whatever you say to me I will give. 12 Ask
me for as great a bride-price and gift as you will, and I will give whatever you
say to me. Only give me the young woman to be my wife."

13 The sons of Jacob answered Shechem and his father Hamor deceitfully,
because he had defiled their sister Dinah. 14 They said to them, "We cannot do
this thing, to give our sister to one who is uncircumcised, for that would be a
disgrace to us. 15 Only on this condition will we agree with you—that you will
become as we are by every male among you being circumcised. 16 Then we will

give our daughters to you, and we will take your daughters to ourselves, and
we will dwell with you and become one people. [17] But if you will not listen to
us and be circumcised, then we will take our daughter, and we will be gone."

[18] Their words pleased Hamor and Hamor's son Shechem. [19] And the young
man did not delay to do the thing, because he delighted in Jacob's daughter.
Now he was the most honored of all his father's house. [20] So Hamor and his
son Shechem came to the gate of their city and spoke to the men of their
city, saying, [21] "These men are at peace with us; let them dwell in the land
and trade in it, for behold, the land is large enough for them. Let us take
their daughters as wives, and let us give them our daughters. [22] Only on this
condition will the men agree to dwell with us to become one people—when
every male among us is circumcised as they are circumcised. [23] Will not their
livestock, their property and all their beasts be ours? Only let us agree with
them, and they will dwell with us." [24] And all who went out of the gate of his
city listened to Hamor and his son Shechem, and every male was circumcised,
all who went out of the gate of his city.

[25] On the third day, when they were sore, two of the sons of Jacob, Simeon
and Levi, Dinah's brothers, took their swords and came against the city while it
felt secure and killed all the males. [26] They killed Hamor and his son Shechem
with the sword and took Dinah out of Shechem's house and went away. [27] The
sons of Jacob came upon the slain and plundered the city, because they had
defiled their sister. [28] They took their flocks and their herds, their donkeys,
and whatever was in the city and in the field. [29] All their wealth, all their little
ones and their wives, all that was in the houses, they captured and plundered.

[30] Then Jacob said to Simeon and Levi, "You have brought trouble on me
by making me stink to the inhabitants of the land, the Canaanites and the
Perizzites. My numbers are few, and if they gather themselves against me
and attack me, I shall be destroyed, both I and my household." [31] But they
said, "Should he treat our sister like a prostitute?"

35:1 God said to Jacob, "Arise, go up to Bethel and dwell there. Make an altar there to the God who appeared to you when you fled from your brother Esau." 2 So Jacob said to his household and to all who were with him, "Put away the foreign gods that are among you and purify yourselves and change your garments. 3 Then let us arise and go up to Bethel, so that I may make there an altar to the God who answers me in the day of my distress and has been with me wherever I have gone." 4 So they gave to Jacob all the foreign gods that they had, and the rings that were in their ears. Jacob hid them under the terebinth tree that was near Shechem.

5 And as they journeyed, a terror from God fell upon the cities that were around them, so that they did not pursue the sons of Jacob. 6 And Jacob came to Luz (that is, Bethel), which is in the land of Canaan, he and all the people who were with him, 7 and there he built an altar and called the place El-bethel, because there God had revealed himself to him when he fled from his brother. 8 And Deborah, Rebekah's nurse, died, and she was buried under an oak below Bethel. So he called its name Allon-bacuth.

9 God appeared to Jacob again, when he came from Paddan-aram, and blessed him. 10 And God said to him, "Your name is Jacob; no longer shall your name be called Jacob, but Israel shall be your name." So he called his name Israel. 11 And God said to him, "I am God Almighty: be fruitful and multiply. A nation and a company of nations shall come from you, and kings shall come from your own body. 12 The land that I gave to Abraham and Isaac I will give to you, and I will give the land to your offspring after you." 13 Then God went up from him in the place where he had spoken with him. 14 And Jacob set up a pillar in the place where he had spoken with him, a pillar of stone. He poured out a drink offering on it and poured oil on it. 15 So Jacob called the name of the place where God had spoken with him Bethel.

16 Then they journeyed from Bethel. When they were still some distance from Ephrath, Rachel went into labor, and she had hard labor. 17 And when

her labor was at its hardest, the midwife said to her, "Do not fear, for you have
another son." [18] And as her soul was departing (for she was dying), she called
his name Ben-oni; but his father called him Benjamin. [19] So Rachel died, and
she was buried on the way to Ephrath (that is, Bethlehem), [20] and Jacob set
up a pillar over her tomb. It is the pillar of Rachel's tomb, which is there to
this day. [21] Israel journeyed on and pitched his tent beyond the tower of Eder.

[22] While Israel lived in that land, Reuben went and lay with Bilhah his
father's concubine. And Israel heard of it.

Now the sons of Jacob were twelve. [23] The sons of Leah: Reuben (Jacob's
firstborn), Simeon, Levi, Judah, Issachar, and Zebulun. [24] The sons of Rachel:
Joseph and Benjamin. [25] The sons of Bilhah, Rachel's servant: Dan and Naphtali. [26] The sons of Zilpah, Leah's servant: Gad and Asher. These were the sons
of Jacob who were born to him in Paddan-aram.

[27] And Jacob came to his father Isaac at Mamre, or Kiriath-arba (that is,
Hebron), where Abraham and Isaac had sojourned. [28] Now the days of Isaac
were 180 years. [29] And Isaac breathed his last, and he died and was gathered
to his people, old and full of days. And his sons Esau and Jacob buried him.

NOTES

OBSERVE: WHAT DOES THE PASSAGE SAY?

Step 1: Setting and Summary

Key Characters and Locations

CHARACTERS:

LOCATIONS:

Summary of the Passage

What Stood Out to You or Piqued Your Curiosity?

Step 2: Key Words and Phrases

NOTES

INTERPRET: WHAT DOES THE PASSAGE MEAN?

Step 3: What Was Hard to Understand?

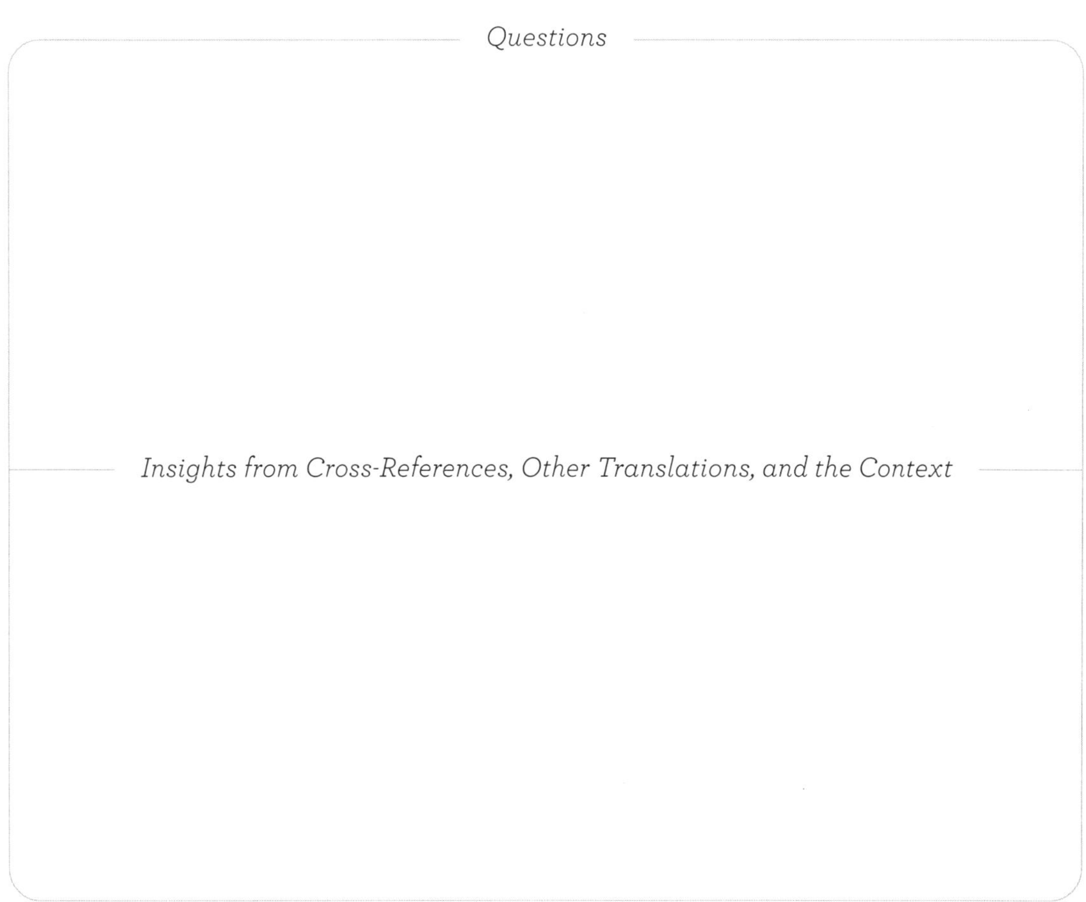

Step 4: What Did You Learn about God?

Refer to the attributes of God in Tool 4 if needed.

NOTES

APPLY: HOW WILL YOU APPLY THE PASSAGE?

Step 5: What Did You Learn about People?

Others

Yourself

Wrap Up: What Did You Discover in the Scriptures That Was Important to You?

7

THE DESCENDANTS OF ESAU AND JACOB'S FAVORITE

Genesis 36:1–8; 37:1–36

THE DESCENDANTS OF ESAU AND JACOB'S FAVORITE

Genesis 36:1–8; 37:1–36

1 These are the generations of Esau (that is, Edom). 2 Esau took his wives from the Canaanites: Adah the daughter of Elon the Hittite, Oholibamah the daughter of Anah the daughter of Zibeon the Hivite, 3 and Basemath, Ishmael's daughter, the sister of Nebaioth. 4 And Adah bore to Esau, Eliphaz; Basemath bore Reuel; 5 and Oholibamah bore Jeush, Jalam, and Korah. These are the sons of Esau who were born to him in the land of Canaan.

6 Then Esau took his wives, his sons, his daughters, and all the members of his household, his livestock, all his beasts, and all his property that he had acquired in the land of Canaan. He went into a land away from his brother Jacob. 7 For their possessions were too great for them to dwell together. The land of their sojournings could not support them because of their livestock. 8 So Esau settled in the hill country of Seir. (Esau is Edom.)

37:1 Jacob lived in the land of his father's sojournings, in the land of Canaan.

2 These are the generations of Jacob.

Joseph, being seventeen years old, was pasturing the flock with his brothers. He was a boy with the sons of Bilhah and Zilpah, his father's wives. And Joseph brought a bad report of them to their father. 3 Now Israel loved Joseph more than any other of his sons, because he was the son of his old age. And he made him a robe of many colors. 4 But when his brothers saw that their father loved him more than all his brothers, they hated him and could not speak peacefully to him.

5 Now Joseph had a dream, and when he told it to his brothers they hated him even more. 6 He said to them, "Hear this dream that I have dreamed: 7 Behold, we were binding sheaves in the field, and behold, my sheaf arose

and stood upright. And behold, your sheaves gathered around it and bowed
down to my sheaf." 8 His brothers said to him, "Are you indeed to reign over
us? Or are you indeed to rule over us?" So they hated him even more for his
dreams and for his words.

9 Then he dreamed another dream and told it to his brothers and said, "Behold, I have dreamed another dream. Behold, the sun, the moon, and eleven
stars were bowing down to me." 10 But when he told it to his father and to his
brothers, his father rebuked him and said to him, "What is this dream that
you have dreamed? Shall I and your mother and your brothers indeed come
to bow ourselves to the ground before you?" 11 And his brothers were jealous
of him, but his father kept the saying in mind.

12 Now his brothers went to pasture their father's flock near Shechem.
13 And Israel said to Joseph, "Are not your brothers pasturing the flock at
Shechem? Come, I will send you to them." And he said to him, "Here I am."
14 So he said to him, "Go now, see if it is well with your brothers and with the
flock, and bring me word." So he sent him from the Valley of Hebron, and
he came to Shechem. 15 And a man found him wandering in the fields. And
the man asked him, "What are you seeking?" 16 "I am seeking my brothers,"
he said. "Tell me, please, where they are pasturing the flock." 17 And the man
said, "They have gone away, for I heard them say, 'Let us go to Dothan.'" So
Joseph went after his brothers and found them at Dothan.

18 They saw him from afar, and before he came near to them they con-
spired against him to kill him. 19 They said to one another, "Here comes this
dreamer. 20 Come now, let us kill him and throw him into one of the pits. Then
we will say that a fierce animal has devoured him, and we will see what will
become of his dreams." 21 But when Reuben heard it, he rescued him out of
their hands, saying, "Let us not take his life." 22 And Reuben said to them,
"Shed no blood; throw him into this pit here in the wilderness, but do not
lay a hand on him"—that he might rescue him out of their hand to restore

him to his father. 23 So when Joseph came to his brothers, they stripped him
of his robe, the robe of many colors that he wore. 24 And they took him and
threw him into a pit. The pit was empty; there was no water in it.

25 Then they sat down to eat. And looking up they saw a caravan of Ishmaelites coming from Gilead, with their camels bearing gum, balm, and myrrh,
on their way to carry it down to Egypt. 26 Then Judah said to his brothers,
"What profit is it if we kill our brother and conceal his blood? 27 Come, let
us sell him to the Ishmaelites, and let not our hand be upon him, for he is
our brother, our own flesh." And his brothers listened to him. 28 Then Midi-
anite traders passed by. And they drew Joseph up and lifted him out of the
pit, and sold him to the Ishmaelites for twenty shekels of silver. They took
Joseph to Egypt.

29 When Reuben returned to the pit and saw that Joseph was not in the pit,
he tore his clothes 30 and returned to his brothers and said, "The boy is gone,
and I, where shall I go?" 31 Then they took Joseph's robe and slaughtered a
goat and dipped the robe in the blood. 32 And they sent the robe of many
colors and brought it to their father and said, "This we have found; please
identify whether it is your son's robe or not." 33 And he identified it and said,
"It is my son's robe. A fierce animal has devoured him. Joseph is without
doubt torn to pieces." 34 Then Jacob tore his garments and put sackcloth
on his loins and mourned for his son many days. 35 All his sons and all his
daughters rose up to comfort him, but he refused to be comforted and said,
"No, I shall go down to Sheol to my son, mourning." Thus his father wept
for him. 36 Meanwhile the Midianites had sold him in Egypt to Potiphar, an
officer of Pharaoh, the captain of the guard.

OBSERVE: WHAT DOES THE PASSAGE SAY?

Step 1: Setting and Summary

Key Characters and Locations

CHARACTERS:

LOCATIONS:

Summary of the Passage

What Stood Out to You or Piqued Your Curiosity?

Step 2: Key Words and Phrases

NOTES

INTERPRET: WHAT DOES THE PASSAGE MEAN?

Step 3: What Was Hard to Understand?

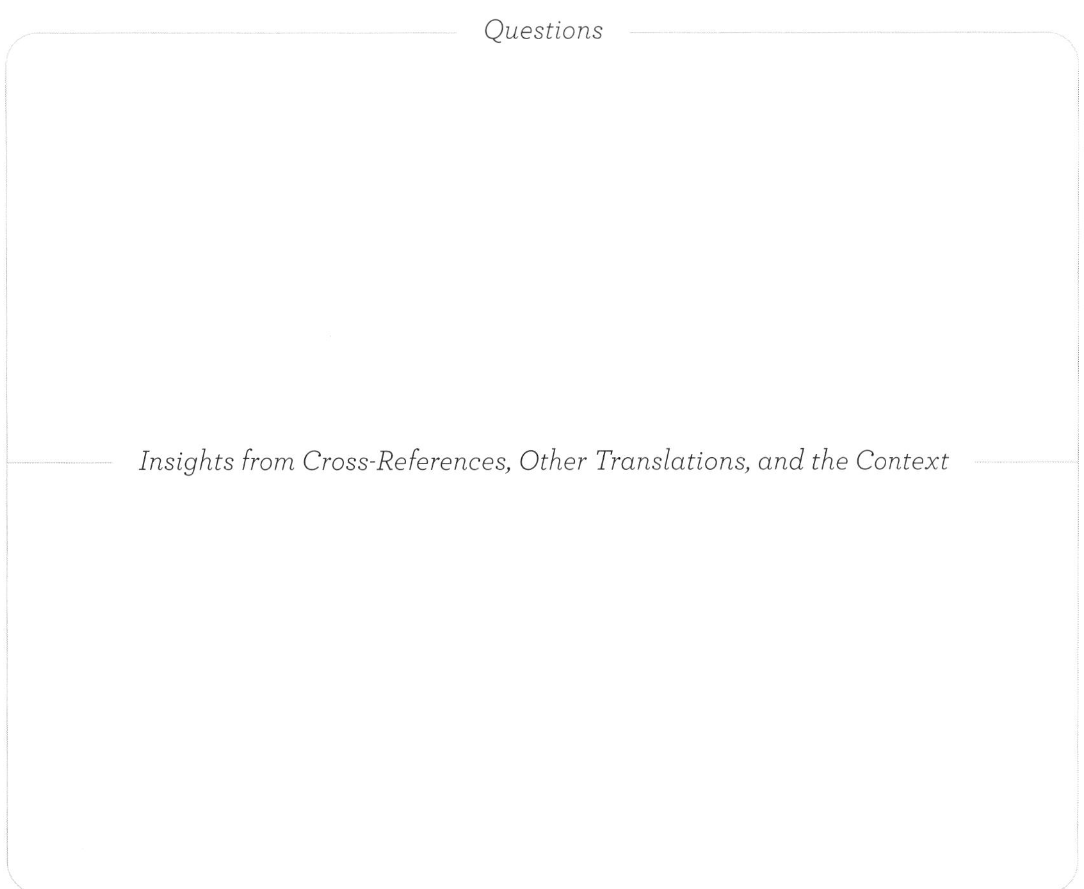

Step 4: What Did You Learn about God?

Refer to the attributes of God in Tool 4 if needed.

NOTES

APPLY: HOW WILL YOU APPLY THE PASSAGE?

Step 5: What Did You Learn about People?

Others

Yourself

Wrap Up: What Did You Discover in the Scriptures That Was Important to You?

8
A REUNION AND RELOCATION FOR JACOB'S DESCENDANTS

Genesis 46:1–34; 47:27–31; 49:28–33

A REUNION AND RELOCATION FOR JACOB'S DESCENDANTS

Genesis 46:1–34; 47:27–31; 49:28–33

Years later, when famine swept the land of Canaan, the nation of Israel (Jacob's family of seventy) moved to Egypt. This was certainly a significant transition in the story of Jacob and in the history of the nation of Israel. The author of Genesis included the names of Jacob's descendants in this part of the story, along with another monumental moment—Jacob's reunion with Joseph.

[1] So Israel took his journey with all that he had and came to Beersheba, and
offered sacrifices to the God of his father Isaac. [2] And God spoke to Israel in
visions of the night and said, "Jacob, Jacob." And he said, "Here I am." [3] Then
he said, "I am God, the God of your father. Do not be afraid to go down to
Egypt, for there I will make you into a great nation. [4] I myself will go down
with you to Egypt, and I will also bring you up again, and Joseph's hand
shall close your eyes."

[5] Then Jacob set out from Beersheba. The sons of Israel carried Jacob
their father, their little ones, and their wives, in the wagons that Pharaoh
had sent to carry him. [6] They also took their livestock and their goods, which
they had gained in the land of Canaan, and came into Egypt, Jacob and all
his offspring with him, [7] his sons, and his sons' sons with him, his daughters,
and his sons' daughters. All his offspring he brought with him into Egypt.

[8] Now these are the names of the descendants of Israel, who came into
Egypt, Jacob and his sons. Reuben, Jacob's firstborn, [9] and the sons of Reuben:
Hanoch, Pallu, Hezron, and Carmi. [10] The sons of Simeon: Jemuel, Jamin,
Ohad, Jachin, Zohar, and Shaul, the son of a Canaanite woman. [11] The sons
of Levi: Gershon, Kohath, and Merari. [12] The sons of Judah: Er, Onan, Shelah,

Perez, and Zerah (but Er and Onan died in the land of Canaan); and the sons
of Perez were Hezron and Hamul. [13] The sons of Issachar: Tola, Puvah, Yob,
and Shimron. [14] The sons of Zebulun: Sered, Elon, and Jahleel. [15] These are
the sons of Leah, whom she bore to Jacob in Paddan-aram, together with his
daughter Dinah; altogether his sons and his daughters numbered thirty-three.

[16] The sons of Gad: Ziphion, Haggi, Shuni, Ezbon, Eri, Arodi, and Areli.
[17] The sons of Asher: Imnah, Ishvah, Ishvi, Beriah, with Serah their sister. And
the sons of Beriah: Heber and Malchiel. [18] These are the sons of Zilpah, whom
Laban gave to Leah his daughter; and these she bore to Jacob—sixteen persons.

[19] The sons of Rachel, Jacob's wife: Joseph and Benjamin. [20] And to Joseph
in the land of Egypt were born Manasseh and Ephraim, whom Asenath, the
daughter of Potiphera the priest of On, bore to him. [21] And the sons of Benjamin: Bela, Becher, Ashbel, Gera, Naaman, Ehi, Rosh, Muppim, Huppim,
and Ard. [22] These are the sons of Rachel, who were born to Jacob—fourteen
persons in all.

[23] The son of Dan: Hushim. [24] The sons of Naphtali: Jahzeel, Guni, Jezer,
and Shillem. [25] These are the sons of Bilhah, whom Laban gave to Rachel his
daughter, and these she bore to Jacob—seven persons in all.

[26] All the persons belonging to Jacob who came into Egypt, who were his
own descendants, not including Jacob's sons' wives, were sixty-six persons
in all. [27] And the sons of Joseph, who were born to him in Egypt, were two.
All the persons of the house of Jacob who came into Egypt were seventy.

[28] He had sent Judah ahead of him to Joseph to show the way before him
in Goshen, and they came into the land of Goshen. [29] Then Joseph prepared
his chariot and went up to meet Israel his father in Goshen. He presented
himself to him and fell on his neck and wept on his neck a good while. [30] Israel
said to Joseph, "Now let me die, since I have seen your face and know that
you are still alive." [31] Joseph said to his brothers and to his father's household, "I will go up and tell Pharaoh and will say to him, 'My brothers and

my father's household, who were in the land of Canaan, have come to me.
32 And the men are shepherds, for they have been keepers of livestock, and
they have brought their flocks and their herds and all that they have.' 33 When
Pharaoh calls you and says, 'What is your occupation?' 34 you shall say, 'Your
servants have been keepers of livestock from our youth even until now, both
we and our fathers,' in order that you may dwell in the land of Goshen, for
every shepherd is an abomination to the Egyptians."

47:27 Thus Israel settled in the land of Egypt, in the land of Goshen. And they
gained possessions in it, and were fruitful and multiplied greatly. 28 And
Jacob lived in the land of Egypt seventeen years. So the days of Jacob, the
years of his life, were 147 years.

29 And when the time drew near that Israel must die, he called his son
Joseph and said to him, "If now I have found favor in your sight, put your
hand under my thigh and promise to deal kindly and truly with me. Do not
bury me in Egypt, 30 but let me lie with my fathers. Carry me out of Egypt
and bury me in their burying place." He answered, "I will do as you have
said." 31 And he said, "Swear to me"; and he swore to him. Then Israel bowed
himself upon the head of his bed.

Note: Although the language of Genesis 47:31 seems to imply that Jacob died, he did not. The NIV reads, "Israel worshiped as he leaned on the top of his staff." Jacob blessed Joseph's sons, Ephraim and Manasseh, before he died. Their blessings are recorded in Genesis 48. Jacob's prophetic blessings to each of his own sons are recorded in Genesis 49. Below is the record of Jacob's death and burial in Genesis 49.

49:28 All these are the twelve tribes of Israel. This is what their father said to
them as he blessed them, blessing each with the blessing suitable to him.
29 Then he commanded them and said to them, "I am to be gathered to my

people; bury me with my fathers in the cave that is in the field of Ephron the
Hittite, 30 in the cave that is in the field at Machpelah, to the east of Mamre, in
the land of Canaan, which Abraham bought with the field from Ephron the
Hittite to possess as a burying place. 31 There they buried Abraham and Sarah
his wife. There they buried Isaac and Rebekah his wife, and there I buried
Leah— 32 the field and the cave that is in it were bought from the Hittites."
33 When Jacob finished commanding his sons, he drew up his feet into the
bed and breathed his last and was gathered to his people.

NOTES

OBSERVE: WHAT DOES THE PASSAGE SAY?

Step 1: Setting and Summary

Key Characters and Locations

CHARACTERS:

LOCATIONS:

Summary of the Passage

What Stood Out to You or Piqued Your Curiosity?

Step 2: Key Words and Phrases

NOTES

INTERPRET: WHAT DOES THE PASSAGE MEAN?

Step 3: What Was Hard to Understand?

Questions

Insights from Cross-References, Other Translations, and the Context

Step 4: What Did You Learn about God?

Refer to the attributes of God in Tool 4 if needed.

NOTES

APPLY: HOW WILL YOU APPLY THE PASSAGE?

Step 5: What Did You Learn about People?

Others

Yourself

Wrap Up: What Did You Discover in the Scriptures That Was Important to You?

MEET ME IN THE BIBLE TOOL KIT

Tool 1

BIBLE TIMELINE

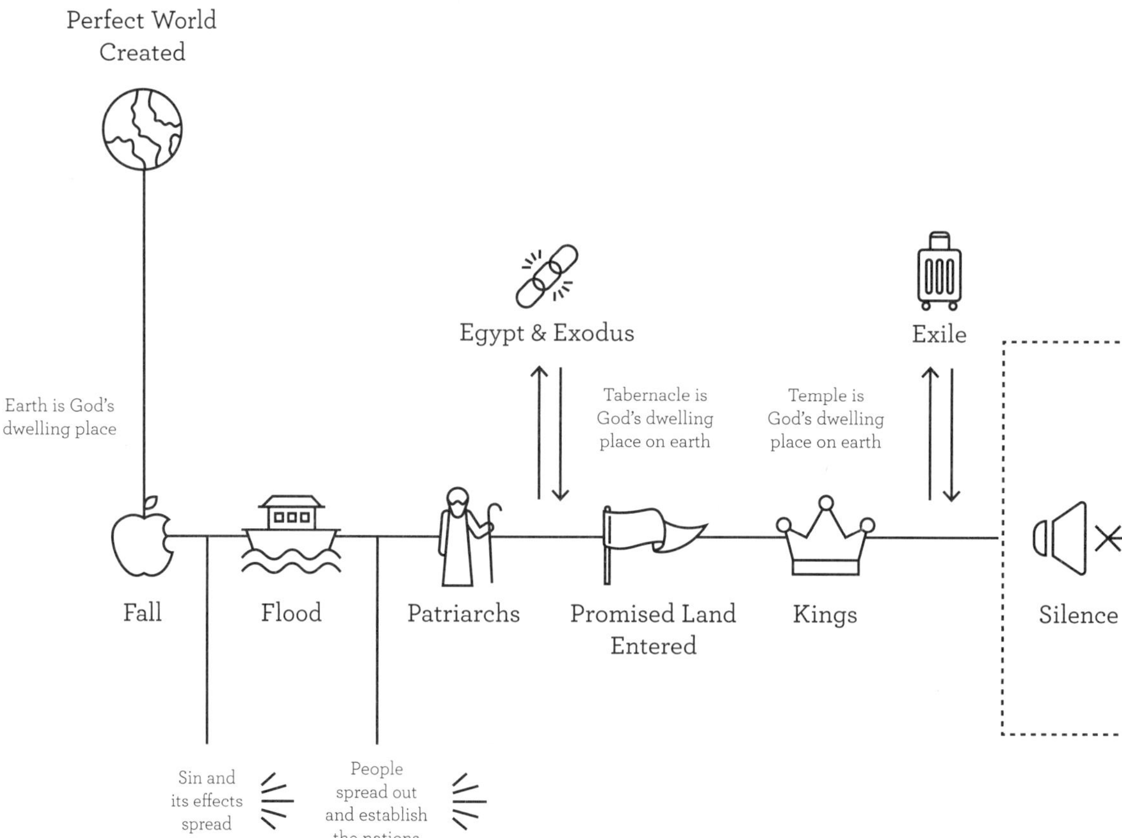

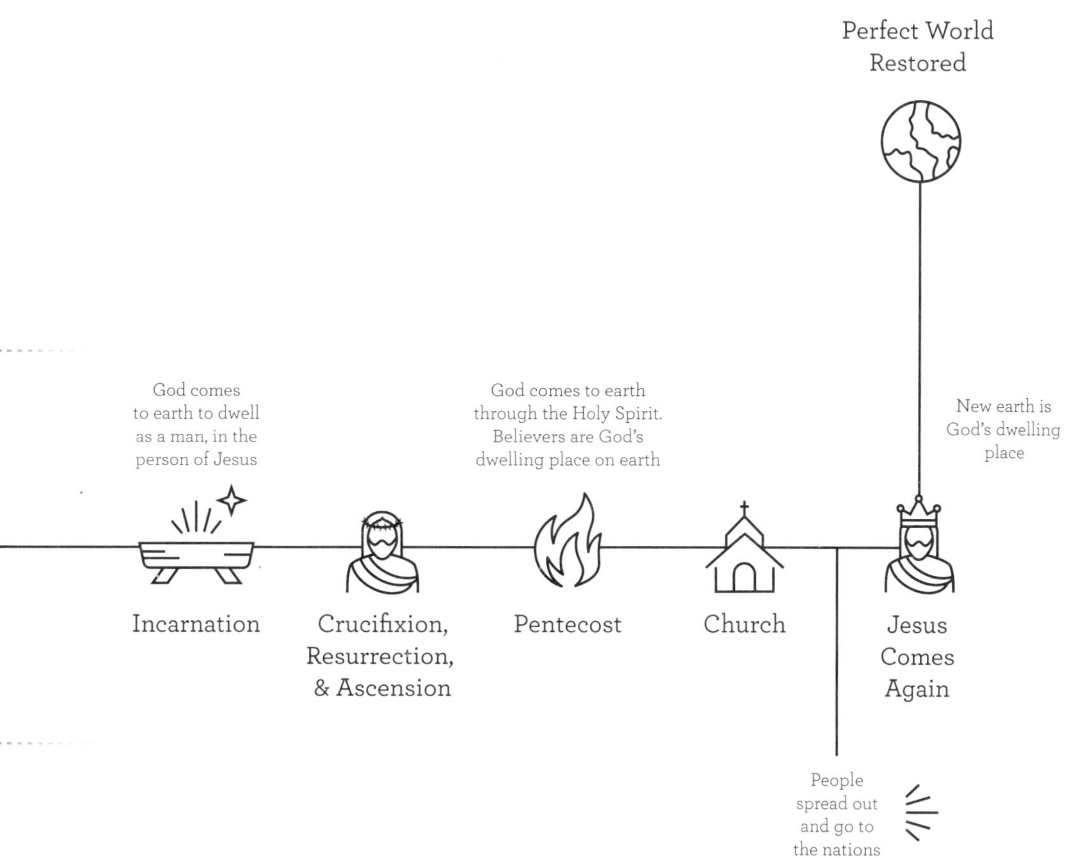
Perfect World
Restored
God comes
to earth to dwell
as a man, in the
person of Jesus
God comes to earth
through the Holy Spirit.
Believers are God's
dwelling place on earth
New earth is
God's dwelling
place
Incarnation
Crucifixion,
Resurrection,
& Ascension
Pentecost
Church
Jesus
Comes
Again
People
spread out
and go to
the nations

Tool 2

MAP: JACOB RETURNS TO CANAAN

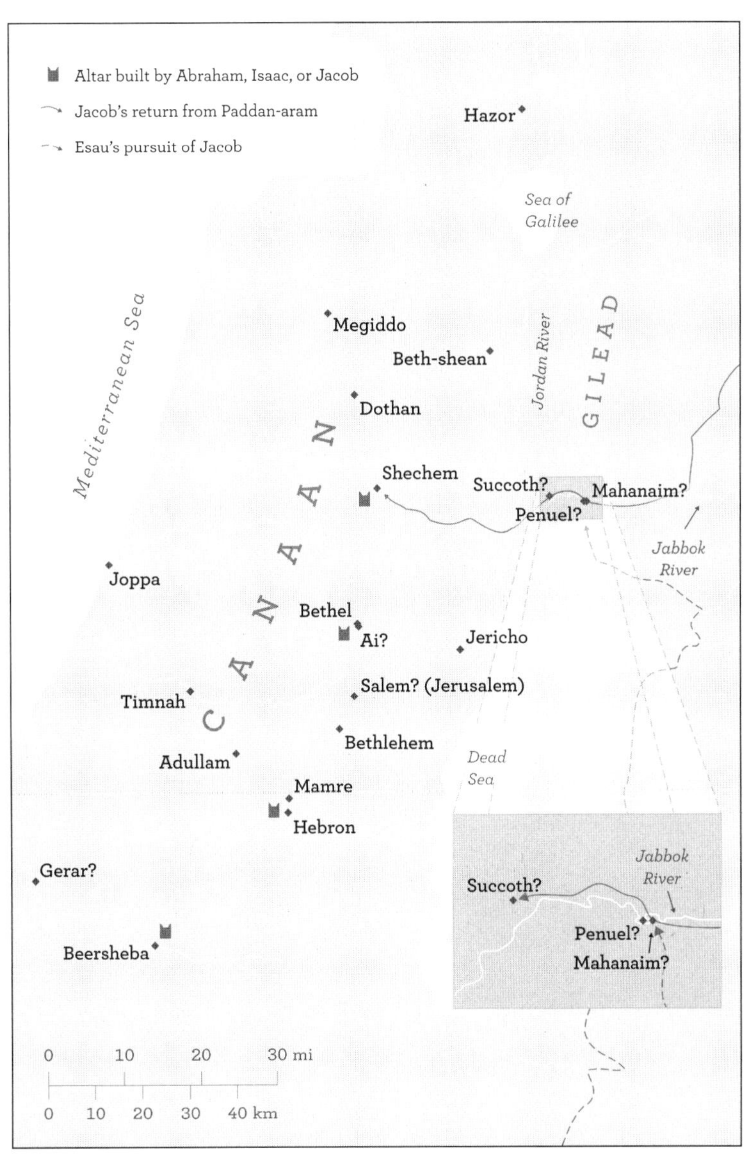

Tool 3

BIBLE GENRES

Knowing the literary style of the book of the Bible you are studying is key to correct interpretation. Just as you would approach the poems of Wordsworth differently than you would approach a history book about World War II, there are nuances to different literary styles in the Bible that must be kept in mind while interpreting and applying the Scriptures. Use this resource to identify the literary style of the book you are studying. Note that several books can be classified in more than one genre.

Genres	Books of the Bible
Apocalyptic. Visionary writings that address future judgment and salvation. Often written using symbolic language.	Daniel, Revelation
Epistle. Letters to Christians in the early church that contain doctrines of the Christian faith and instructions for Christlike living.	Romans, 1–2 Corinthians, Galatians, Ephesians, Philippians, Colossians, 1–2 Thessalonians, 1–2 Timothy, Titus, Philemon, Hebrews, James, 1–2 Peter, 1–3 John, Jude
Gospel. Historical narratives that give testimony to the genealogy, birth, life, death, resurrection, and teachings of Jesus Christ. Each Gospel is written by a different author from a different perspective and with a different emphasis.	Matthew, Mark, Luke, John

Genres	Books of the Bible
Historical Narrative. Narrations of the factual history of Israel and the early church. Historical narratives are recordings of what happened, not necessarily what should have happened had people obeyed God's commands.	Genesis, Exodus, Leviticus, Numbers, Deuteronomy, Joshua, Judges, Ruth, 1–2 Samuel, 1–2 Kings, 1–2 Chronicles, Ezra, Nehemiah, Esther, Jonah, Acts
Poetry. Expressions of joy, thanksgiving, celebration, disappointment, anxiety, and lament in poetic forms.	Psalms, Song of Solomon, Lamentations
Prophecy. God's message to his people spoken through prophets, calling God's people to repentance from sin, warning them of judgment, and revealing events yet to come.	Isaiah, Jeremiah, Ezekiel, Daniel, Hosea, Joel, Amos, Obadiah, Jonah, Micah, Nahum, Habakkuk, Zephaniah, Haggai, Zechariah, Malachi
Wisdom Literature. Writings that address life's basic questions about what it means to live faithful, God-centered lives in both big crises and everyday circumstances.	Job, some Psalms, Proverbs, Ecclesiastes

Tool 4

ATTRIBUTES OF GOD

Attentive. God hears and responds to the needs of his children.

Compassionate. God cares for his children and acts on their behalf.

Creator. God made everything. He is uncreated.

Deliverer. God rescues and saves his children.

Eternal. God is not limited by and exists outside of time.

Faithful. God always keeps his promises.

Generous. God gives what is best and beyond what is deserved.

Glorious. God displays his greatness and worth.

Good. God is what is best and gives what is best.

Holy. God is perfect, pure, and without sin.

Immutable/Unchanging. God never changes. He is the same yesterday, today, and tomorrow.

Incomprehensible. God is beyond our understanding. We can comprehend him in part but not in whole.

Infinite. God has no limits in his person or on his power.

Jealous. God will not share his glory with another. All glory rightfully belongs to him.

Just. God is fair in all his actions and judgments. He cannot overpunish or underpunish.

Loving. God feels and displays infinite, unconditional affection toward his children. His love for them does not depend on their worth, their response, or their merit.

Merciful. God does not give his children the punishment they deserve.

Omnipotent/Almighty. God holds all power. Nothing is too hard for God. What he wills he can accomplish.

Omnipresent. God is fully present everywhere.

Omniscient. God knows everything past, present, and future, all potential and real outcomes, all things micro and macro.

Patient/Long-Suffering. God is untiring and bears with his children.

Provider. God meets the needs of his children.

Refuge. God is a place of safety and protection for his children.

Righteous. God is always good and right.

Self-Existent. God depends on nothing and no one to give him life or existence.

Sovereign. God does everything according to his plan and pleasure. He controls all things.

Transcendent. God is not like humans. He is infinitely higher in being and action.

Truthful. Whatever God speaks or does is truth and reality.

Wise. God knows what is best and acts accordingly. He cannot choose wrongly.

Worthy. God deserves all glory and honor and praise.

Wrathful. God hates all unrighteousness.

Tool 5

BOOKMARK CONTENT

Begin by asking God to reveal himself as you read the Scriptures. Enjoy him and have fun learning and discovering!

Observe: What Does the Passage Say?

Step 1. Setting and Summary

- Read the passage, noting key characters and locations.
- Write a brief summary of the passage (about three to five sentences).
- Record what stood out to you or piqued your curiosity.

Step 2. Key Words and Phrases

- Read the passage, marking the words/phrases that are repeated or emphasized.
- Why do you think the author repeats these words? Look back at the context to help you with your answer (e.g., Who wrote it and to whom was it written?). Write down your insights.
- Are there words for which you need a better understanding (e.g., *propitiation, atonement*)? Use a dictionary or thesaurus to gain insight and note what you discover.
- Read the verses with key words/phrases in two other Bible translations. Jot down what you learn.
- Enjoy God. Talk to him and listen.

Interpret: What Does the Passage Mean?

Step 3. What Was Hard to Understand?

- Read the passage, writing down the questions that surface for you.

- Record insights you gain from the following:
    - Looking up cross-references for verses that are hard to understand.
    - Reading the passage in two other Bible translations.
    - Looking back at the context (e.g., Who wrote it and to whom was it written and when?).

Step 4. What Did You Learn about God?

- What attribute of God stood out to you in this passage?
- How does this attribute of God encourage you to anchor your hope in him? Record your discoveries.
- Enjoy God. Talk to him and listen.

Apply: How Will You Apply the Passage?

Step 5. What Did You Learn about People?

OTHERS

- What did you learn about people in this passage? How does this passage promote a love for others? Write down your thoughts.
- What did you learn that you can share with others (a friend, coworker, family member)? Pray for meaningful conversations this week.

YOURSELF

- Is there a command to obey? An example to follow? A sin to confess? A warning to heed? An encouragement to receive? Record your insights.
- What action step will you take? How will next week be different because you chose to apply what you discovered?
- Enjoy God. Talk to him and listen.

Tool 6

PRAYER PAGES

PRAYER PAGE

PRAYER PAGE

PRAYER PAGE

PRAYER PAGE

PRAYER PAGE

PRAYER PAGE

PRAYER PAGE

Tool 7

QUESTIONS FOR FURTHER THOUGHT AND DISCUSSION

These questions were written to help you think deeply about the text. Additional historical context is also given. Many questions do not have one right answer and are meant to encourage further thought and robust discussion. The bounce questions are intended to jumpstart discussion and provide an easy transition to the content.

Discussion leaders may use as many or as few questions as they'd like. The prompts on your bookmark also make good points of discussion.

Getting Started in the Story of Jacob

1. Why do you want to study the story of Jacob?
2. As you answered the context questions found in "Getting Started in the Story of Jacob," what new insight did you gain?
3. What piqued your curiosity?
4. Complete the sentence: At the end of this study, I hope to ____________.

Jacob Wrestles with Esau (Genesis 25:19–26:35)

Helpful Context

- Jacob's name literally means "the one who cheats."
- Scripture does not state if Abimelech of Genesis 26 is the same man or a descendant of the Abimelech in Genesis 20. He is most likely a descendant.

Discussion Questions

- Bounce question: What nickname were you given when you were growing up? Did you like it? Why or why not?

1. Think back to the story of Abraham and Sarah, Isaac's parents (see Gen. 11:30; 16:1). What did Sarah and Rebekah have in common? What was different about their experiences?
2. What was the significance of the birthright? In other words, what was Esau willing to give up for the bowl of stew? What did you learn about Esau from this passage?
3. In what way(s) might we be tempted to treat our inheritance in Christ too lightly?
4. What did you learn about Jacob from this passage?
5. Review Genesis 20 regarding Abraham and Abimelech. What did Isaac assume about Abimelech? What can we learn about how to engage people of other faiths and cultures from this passage?
6. There are a number of wells mentioned in Genesis 26. Why do you think the redigging of Abraham's wells is significant? (See Gen. 26:22 for insight.)
7. What did you learn about God in Genesis 25 and 26? In what ways were you encouraged by these scriptures?

Jacob Deceives, God Promises (Genesis 27:1–28:22)

Helpful Context

- Notice the steps Jacob and Rebekah took to trick Isaac into believing that Jacob was the eldest son, Esau. Keep these in mind and note the parallels when you read about how Laban tricked Jacob into marrying his eldest daughter, Leah.
- Jacob responded to the dream God gave him by setting up a pillar and making a vow, recorded in Genesis 28:18–22. He eventually

traveled back to this place years later. When Jacob returned, he had failed multiple times, but God had upheld all that he said.

Discussion Questions

- Bounce question: Think back to a time when you were impacted by favoritism. Were you the favorite grandchild? Teacher's pet? Describe how it felt.

1. What did Jacob do to secure Isaac's blessing? What was Rebekah's role?
2. Do you think Rebekah was acting in obedience to what God had spoken to her (Gen. 25:22–23)? Why or why not?
3. In what areas of your life are you tempted to "help" God keep his promises?
4. Why do you think God chose Jacob to be the patriarch? Was it because of Jacob's strength? His character? In what way(s) are you encouraged by this?
5. In what way(s) should we be warned by Jacob's actions?
6. Which key character did you most relate to: Isaac, Esau, Rebekah, or Jacob? How so?
7. Review Genesis 28:6–9. How did Esau react to his plight? What do you think about this?
8. What did you learn about people in these chapters?
9. Name one way you have observed God's faithfulness to you over the years, regardless of your behavior.

Jacob, Leah, and Rachel (Genesis 29:1–30:24)

Helpful Context

- In Genesis 29:13 we read that Jacob told Laban "all these things." Then Laban replied with an enthusiastic, "Surely you are my bone and my flesh!" (v. 14). This was an odd response considering that Jacob had likely explained how he had inherited his father's wealth, though not the firstborn. We are first introduced to Laban in Genesis 24 when Abraham's servant met Rebekah. Read Genesis 24:28–31 to gain insight about Laban. Keep these things in mind as you read his story.

- In Genesis 30, you read about mandrakes. Mandrakes are a type of Mediterranean plant thought to have magical powers. Some thought that mandrakes increased fertility, while some thought the plant to be an aphrodisiac. Keep this in mind while reading Genesis 30:14–18. Imagine the desperation of Leah and Rachel while you read this part of their story.

Discussion Questions

- Bounce question: Do you believe in love at first sight? Why or why not?

1. Notice how Jacob responded when he met Rachel: he wept loudly. Why do you think this is?
2. Jacob offered to serve Laban for seven years to secure Rachel as his bride. This was an exorbitant bride price. Why do you think he offered this rather than an expected length of service? What insight do you gain about Jacob?
3. Think back to Genesis 27 and compare the similarities between Jacob's deception of Isaac and Laban's deception of Jacob. Why do you think Laban deceived Jacob in this way? What did Laban have to gain?
4. What choice did Jacob have to make after he woke up next to Leah? Do you think God was pleased with his choice? How did his choice affect Leah and Rachel?
5. What did you learn about Leah through the names of her sons? What is the implication of Leah being the mother of Judah (Matt. 1:1–3)?
6. What did you learn about God through his response to Leah? Through his response to Rachel? Did God have a favorite? How does their story help you anchor your hope in God in your current circumstances?

Jacob Wrestles with Laban (Genesis 30:25–31:55)

Helpful Context

- This passage is fascinating and a bit confusing. The common, though faulty, belief of the day regarding genetics was that what animals looked at while they mated directly affected the physical traits of their offspring. Jacob whittled sticks to create stripes, the dark bark of the stick alternating with stripes of the white flesh underneath the bark. He placed the striped, multicolored sticks in front of the strongest animals in order to produce strong, multicolored offspring. This would leave weaker, solid-colored offspring for Laban.
- The dream described in Genesis 31:10–13 was given to Jacob prior to the activity of striping sticks and placing them in front of the strongest animals.
- Jacob's mother, Rebekah, was also spoken to by God, knowing the end result beforehand (Gen. 25:22–24).

Discussion Questions

- Bounce question: Describe a time when you did more than necessary in order to get ahead.

1. Did Jacob need to whittle sticks in order to prosper? Do you think Jacob was acting in obedience to the dream God gave him? Why or why not? Compare Jacob's actions in this passage with his mother's actions in Genesis 27:5–17.
2. Name a way that God has miraculously provided for you in the past.
3. In what way(s) might we be guilty of striping sticks?
4. The scheming and deceiving in Genesis 30 and 31 are exhausting. Of the deceptions named in these chapters, which one surprised you most?
5. Why do you think Rachel took the household gods to her new homeland?

6. Why do you think God referred to himself as "the God of Bethel" in 31:13? What did Jacob learn about God through his experience with Laban?
7. What seemed important to you in the story of Jacob "wrestling" with Laban?

Jacob Wrestles with God (Genesis 32:1–33:20)

Helpful Context

- We tend to believe that it would be easier to trust God if he spoke to us through angels and dreams and blessed us with supernatural prosperity. Look back through Jacob's story so far to count how many dreams and supernatural encounters he had.
- Remember: Jacob's name means "the one who cheats."

Discussion Questions

- Bounce question: Describe a sweet yet unexpected reunion you have experienced.

1. Jacob's scheming ways did not stop. What did he assume about Esau? What was his scheme (32:6–8)?
2. Think about each of Jacob's schemes so far:
    - Dressing up as Esau.
    - Striping sticks to prosper his flocks.
    - Dividing his family and livestock into two camps and sending them ahead.
    - Leading Esau to think he would join him in Seir, but traveling to Succoth instead.

    What do all have in common?
3. At what point during the all-night wrestling match do you think Jacob realized who he was wrestling with?

4. Read Genesis 32:26–28 below, filling in the blanks with "the one who cheats."

   > Then he said, "Let me go, for the day has broken." But Jacob said, "I will not let you go unless you bless me." And he said to him, "What is your name?" And he said, "I am ______________." Then he said, "Your name shall no longer be called ______________, but Israel, for you have striven with God and with men, and have prevailed."

5. Why do you think God chose to engage Jacob by wrestling with him all night? Think back to how Jacob's life began, even in his mother's womb.

6. What did you learn about God as you studied Jacob and Esau's reunion?

The Tragedy of Dinah and a Name Change for Jacob (Genesis 34:1–35:29)

Helpful Context

- Circumcision was the mark of the covenant, chosen by God and commanded by God. Flesh was torn and blood was shed as a sobering reminder of God's binding agreement with Abraham's descendants. This mark of the covenant also served to set apart the people of Israel. Keep this in mind as you consider Simeon and Levi's revenge.

- God renamed Jacob again in Genesis 35. Be sure to note the location of the renaming and the restating by God of his covenant with Abraham, Isaac, and now Jacob.

Discussion Questions

- Bounce question: What does your name mean?

1. The reunion of Esau and Jacob was bittersweet because Jacob let us down again. Review 33:18–19. Where did Jacob pitch his tent? Now look at the map in Tool 2 of the Tool Kit and locate Shechem. Then find Bethel. He was not where he was supposed to be (see Gen. 31:11–13),

and Dinah suffered greatly as a result. Does this remind you of another Old Testament leader? What is the warning for us?

2. Neither Jacob nor his sons, Simeon and Levi, responded rightly after the rape of Dinah. What was Jacob's failure?
3. Review 34:13. In what way did Jacob's sons behave like him?
4. Do you think Shechem and his city received justice at the hands of Simeon and Levi? Why or why not?
5. What evidence do we see in the text that God was deeply grieved by the rape of Dinah? What evidence have you observed in the story of Jacob that God sees and values women, although the culture at the time did not?
6. Name the changes that took place before God renamed Jacob a second time (see Gen. 35:1–3). Why do you think God renamed Jacob a second time?
7. Why do you think the Holy Spirit inspired Moses to record such disheartening events in the Bible?

The Descendants of Esau and Jacob's Favorite (Genesis 36:1–8; 37:1–36)

Helpful Context

- Genesis 36:6–7 sounds similar to the physical separation between Abram and Lot, recorded in Genesis 13:2–6. Two separate people groups have begun.
- Think back to the story of Leah, Rachel, their servants Bilhah and Zilpah, and all of the sons (see especially Gen. 33:1–3). Consider what incited the hatred toward Joseph even before he received his special robe.
- Notice that the names Jacob and Israel are used interchangeably in the text.

Discussion Questions

- Bounce question: Why do you think sibling rivalry is a common struggle?

1. Whose name do you recognize in 36:1–3? What do you learn about Esau in these verses?
2. Name the ways that the sons of Jacob were still feeling the effects of Jacob's overt favoritism toward Rachel and her son Joseph.
3. Do you think Joseph was wrong to share his dreams with his brothers?
4. Why do you think the author used both names for the father, sometimes using the name Jacob and other times using the name Israel? The interchange of both names continues throughout the Old Testament. Why do you think this is?
5. What characteristics of the eldest son does Reuben exhibit? Which brother do the others follow (37:26)? Why do you think this is? See Genesis 34:30 and 35:22 for help.
6. Jacob wrestled with his twin brother, his father-in-law, and even God. Chapter 37 records his struggle with his sons. What do the actions of the brothers communicate about their feelings toward their father, Jacob?
7. Imagine being Joseph in this scenario. How would you have felt?

A Reunion and Relocation for Jacob's Descendants (Genesis 46:1–34; 47:27–31; 49:28–33)

Helpful Context

- There is a difference between the twelve sons of Jacob named in Genesis 49 and the twelve tribes of Israel under Moses (Num. 2:1–34). The twelve tribes of Israel are as follows: Reuben, Simeon, Judah, Dan, Naphtali, Gad, Asher, Issachar, Zebulun, Benjamin, Ephraim, and Manasseh. Although no tribe bore the name of Joseph, two tribes,

Ephraim and Manasseh, were named after Joseph's sons. The descendants of Levi had a special calling to hold the priesthood. Because of this calling, they lived among the other tribes.

Discussion Questions

- Bounce question: Have you had to relocate due to circumstances beyond your control? What was that like?

1. Why do you think God told Jacob not to be afraid to go down to Egypt? See Genesis 12:10–20 for help.
2. Look back at Genesis 26:23–25 and 28:12–15. What evidence do you see in Jacob's story that God makes covenants and keeps them?
3. Notice who Jacob is buried next to in Genesis 49:31–32. Does this surprise you? Throughout the pages of the Bible, we observe that God often chooses the one who is unexpected. How is this demonstrated through Leah?
4. It was important to Abraham that Sarah was buried in Canaan (see Gen. 23). What is significant about Jacob also being buried in Canaan alongside Abraham and Isaac?
5. In what ways is Jacob/Israel a right representative of the nation of Israel throughout the rest of the Old Testament?
6. Genesis is a book of beginnings. What beginnings did you read about in the story of Jacob?
7. What did you learn through the story of Jacob that you hope to never forget?

NOTES

1. My favorite tool is *Merriam-Webster's Collegiate Dictionary*, 11th ed. (Springfield, MA: Merriam-Webster, 2003), continually updated at https://www.merriam-webster.com.
2. I demonstrate how to use Bible Gateway (https://www.biblegateway.com/) to cross-reference in my introductory video: https://www.colleensearcy.com/.
3. Bible Gateway (https://www.biblegateway.com/) also includes footnotes.
4. I've found Tim Challies's article helpful: "Best Commentaries on Each Book of the Bible," Challies website, accessed April 29, 2024, https://challies.com/.
5. Questions 1–4 are informed by Jen Wilkin, *Women of the Word: How to Study the Bible with Both Our Hearts and Our Minds* (Wheaton, IL: Crossway, 2014).
6. For further study on Bible genres, a helpful resource is Gordon D. Fee and Douglas Stuart, *How to Read the Bible for All Its Worth* (Grand Rapids, MI: Zondervan, 2014).

Meet Me in the Bible

For more information, visit **crossway.org**.